Computer Monographs

GENERAL EDITOR: Stanley Gill, M.A., Ph.D.

ASSOCIATE EDITOR: J. J. Florentin, Ph.D., Imperial College, London.

Assemblers and Loaders

Assemblers and Loaders

D. W. BARRON
Professor of Computation
University of Southampton

Second Edition

Macdonald · London and
American Elsevier Inc. · New York

© D. W. Barron 1969, 1972

First Published 1969
Second Impression 1970
Third Impression 1971
Second Edition 1972

Sole distributors for the British Isles and Commonwealth
Macdonald & Co. (Publishers) Ltd.
P.O. Box 2 L.G., 49–50 Poland Street, London W.1

Sole distributors for the United States and Dependencies
American Elsevier Publishing Company, Inc.
52 Vanderbilt Avenue, New York, N.Y. 10017

All remaining areas
Elsevier Publishing Company
P.O. Box 211, Jan van Galenstraat 335, Amsterdam, The Netherlands

British Standard Book Number SBN 356 04014 3
American Standard Book Number ISBN 0 444 19585 8
Library of Congress Catalog Card Number 78 171220

Made and printed in Great Britain by
Hazell Watson & Viney Ltd., Aylesbury, Bucks.

Contents

Preface

Assemblers and loaders have received little attention in the literature, being overshadowed by the more spectacular topic of compilers. However, their study makes an excellent introduction to advanced programming for the student of computer science, or the professional programmer who is interested in what goes on behind the scenes. Assemblers and loaders introduce, in a simple framework, ideas and techniques which occur in more complicated forms in compilers and other software.

This monograph is concerned with the design and implementation of assemblers and loaders. It is not a highly detailed treatise on the subject, but aims to give an understanding of the principles and a general appreciation of the techniques used, sufficient to form a basis for the study of any actual assembly system that the user may encounter. Some knowledge of computers and programming is assumed of the reader. Wherever possible I have acknowledged the source of material used, but much of what appears in the book is part of the lore of software programming that has hitherto been passed on by word of mouth. One has only to examine some commercially available assemblers to see how uneven the process of information dissemination has been, and I hope that this attempt to set down a small part of the accumulated know-how will serve a useful purpose.

Southampton, 1968 D. W. Barron

Preface to the Second Edition

The most noticeable change in this second edition is the inclusion of a greatly expanded Chapter 8 on Meta-Assemblers, and an entirely new Chapter 9 on Algol-like Assemblers. However, I have taken the opportunity to make extensive revisions throughout the book. Some of these involve new material, others are merely attempts to improve the clarity of exposition. I hope that my readers will feel that I have been successful in this endeavour.

Southampton 1971.   D. W. Barron

Acknowledgement

The author acknowledges the permission of International Computers Ltd to use certain ICL material in this publication. Save for such permission all copyright, patent and intellectual property rights belong to ICL.

1 Why and how

What is an assembler? Like many other things in computing it is difficult to define precisely, though any experienced programmer will recognise one when he sees it. An assembler (or more correctly, a symbolic assembly program) is a system that assists the programmer in the preparation of machine-code programs. A program as executed by the processor consists usually of binary information in consecutive registers of the core store. The assembler allows the programmer to write symbolic representations of the contents of store registers, and converts these into binary words. It also does the tedious 'book-keeping', keeping track of cross-references within the program, and facilitates the combining of subprograms to form larger programs. If we use the term *machine language* to mean binary patterns interpreted by the processor hardware, then an assembler takes programs written in *symbolic assembly language* and translates them into machine language: it is thus in some sense a compiler. The distinction between an assembler and a compiler is a difficult one to make. A simple, though inadequate, distinction is to define an assembler as a translation program in which there is a one-to-one correspondence between the lines of the source program and the machine instructions generated. This, however, excludes macro assemblers.

A better distinction is to say that assemblers translate *machine-oriented* languages, whilst compilers translate *problem-oriented* languages; but even this distinction breaks down in some cases (see Chapter 9). This book takes the view that an assembler processes a program in which the written instructions mirror the internal structure of the machine, i.e. they are symbolic representations of the contents of store registers or groups of registers, and allow the programmer direct reference to internal function codes, accumulators, index registers, etc. A slightly different definition is that an assembly language is a language in which the data structure is the registers and store of a computer, and the permitted operations parallel the machine code operations of that computer. An assembler is then a compiler for such an assembly language.

The need for assemblers and loaders arises from the fact that the computer requires its instructions to be in the form of groups of binary digits, whilst the programmer likes to use alphabetical symbols and decimal numbers. It was not always obvious that this preference on the part of the programmers should be indulged, and in the early days there were those who argued that programs should be presented in a form as near as possible to the internal binary format. This dichotomy of opinion was exemplified by two of the earliest machines, the Manchester Mark I and the EDSAC 1. The EDSAC incorporated an assembler and instructions were written with a single letter function code, a decimal address, and a terminating code letter which provided relative addressing, and a primitive sort of symbolic addressing. The Manchester machine, on the other hand, required programs to be prepared with each instruction represented by four base-32 characters. These characters were chosen so that when punched on 5-track paper tape the four tape rows, when concatenated, gave the correct binary pattern for the instruction. This leads to some bizarre results, for since address-modification was indicated by a high-order bit in the instruction, an 'add' instruction, for example, was not represented by a unique character, thus making programs difficult to read.* Programmer convenience won the day, and more and more facilities were added to assemblers, including the ability to refer to storage locations by symbolic name, to use such names before storage has been allocated, to use literal operands, etc.

A further line of development arose out of the increasing size of programs, and the increasing use of library subroutines. A long program is best developed by breaking it up into a number of more or less independent *subprograms* or *routines*† which can be written

* The difference in philosophy between the Manchester and the Cambridge approach may have resulted from the different operation of the input instruction. The Manchester machine had an input instruction which read four rows of tape and assembled them as a binary word, whereas the EDSAC input instruction read a single tape row. There was thus a built-in incentive on the Manchester machine to use a binary program input.

† Some systems use the name segment for our subprogram. In view of hardware connotations of the word segment we will not follow this usage.

and tested separately. There will of course be cross-references between routines, and the details of these will not be known at the time the routines are written. There is thus a requirement for a system which will make up a program out of a set of routines and library programs, keeping track of all the cross-references and filling these in so as to produce a program ready to run. Hence the name assembly program.*

The simplest assemblers are the *load-and-go* variety. They take a program in symbolic form, complete except possibly for library routines, assemble it in binary in the core store, then immediately enter it. This is usually achieved by making one scan of the source program, in which case the assembler is described as a *one-pass* system. Although there is no question of making up a program out of subprograms, a load-and-go assembler can provide for the automatic incorporation of any library routines that have been referred to. The advantages to be gained from breaking up a large program into more or less independent routines have already been noted. Besides the convenience to the programmer of allowing him to concentrate on logically independent units, there may be a gain in efficiency, since if a program is changed, only the routine(s) containing the changes(s) need to be reassembled. Further, since the work in processing cross-references is roughly proportional to the square of the number of instructions in the program, there is a reduction in the amount of work to be done at assembly time. Most assemblers, therefore, are *routine* (or *subprogram*) *assemblers*.

Such assemblers produce the assembled form of the routine on some external medium, in a form suitable for later combination with other routines. They generally work on a *two-pass* basis, that is, they make two scans of the source program. The first pass builds up a *symbol table* by collecting together all the symbol definitions (explicit or implicit) in the routine, and the second pass does the actual translation, using the symbol values accumulated in the first pass. The assembler must distinguish three sorts of information in the source program. First there are those items, such as operation codes

---

* It is interesting to note that this requirement was recognised by the designers of the EDSAC 1, who provided library programs to organise the incorporation of library subroutines. That this did not catch on with the users of the EDSAC was probably due to the fact that in the absence of any backing store, programs had to be physically assembled on to a paper tape, and with a store of only 512 words it was not possible to write a very big program anyway.

and numerical constants, that have a value which does not depend on the position of the routine in the store. They are thus independent of the way this routine is combined with other routines, and are said to be *absolute* quantities. Then there are symbols which name instructions or working stores within the routine, which are not referred to by other routines. Although the actual store address of such items will depend on the position of the routine in the store, and hence on the way in which it is combined with other routines, the position relative to the start of the routine is known uniquely. Such information is said to be *relocatable,* since it is only necessary to add a datum corresponding to the start of the routine in store to produce an absolute address. Finally there are the cross-reference symbols which are defined and/or referred to in other routines, whose values are unknown until the whole program is put together.

The assembler produces its output in *binary-symbolic* or *semicompiled* form. The program is converted into binary (absolute or relocatable as appropriate) except for the cross-reference symbols, which are retained (of necessity) in symbolic form. The assembler produces with each routine relocation information, showing where relocatable addresses have been used, and tables of the use of global (external) symbols in the routine. Such binary-symbolic routines are combined into a program, possibly together with library subroutines (which are also stored in semicompiled form), by a linkage editor or linking loader, which are described in detail in Chapter 5.

In brief, a linking loader takes as its input a sequence of binary symbolic routines. As each routine is encountered, the loader first notes the address into which the first instruction will be loaded; this is the datum for the routine. The routine is then loaded, and the relocation information is used to adjust relative addresses by adding the datum. The datum is then adjusted in readiness for the next routine. The loader keeps track of the cross-reference symbols as they are defined. If at the end of loading any of these symbols remains undefined, this can be used to initiate a scan of the library, so that library routines that have been called will automatically be incorporated into the program. This is one of the many ways in which an assembler/loader combination relieves the programmer of unwanted chores.

The loader as described carries out two operations that are

logically distinct, these being the linking of subprograms on the one hand, and relocation on the other. In the context of a modern operating system in which programs can be stored on disc, it is usual to separate these functions. Linking of subprograms is achieved by a *linkage editor* or *consolidator*; the output from this is a program entirely in relocatable binary, which can be stored and later loaded into core by a relocating loader prior to execution. A consequence of this method of working is that the programmer does not have control over the location in store of the various parts of his program and its data. This is not in general important, however. Indeed, given adequate diagnostics (a requirement all too rarely satisfied) there is in most cases no need for the programmer to know the absolute addresses of his programs and data.

A further advantage of this system of working is that once there exists a linkage editor which will combine previously assembled subprograms, it is in principle possible for the subprograms to be written in different source languages, provided that the assemblers/compilers produce the same binary-symbolic format. However, before this is a workable proposition it is necessary to standardise the calling sequence by which subroutines are entered.

The method of working described above, involving independent compiling, linkage editing and relocation is employed almost universally nowadays on all except the smallest machines, both for assemblers and for compilers. Indeed, many programmers would take the view that it is the obvious, and only, way to do the job. It is therefore worth looking at the reasons why this approach was adopted, and seeing if the arguments are still valid in the context of present day hardware. The most quoted benefit is that when a program is changed, only those routines that have actually been altered need to be recompiled. This assumes that compiling is slow and linkage editing/relocation is fast. If, as is often the case, the linkage editing and relocation are the dominant factors in the time taken (as is often the case) then the gain from selective recompiling is illusory. A second benefit is the automatic incorporation of routines from libraries. But this could be done just as well with libraries in source form. Again, it is often thought that semi-compiled form is a compact way of storing a routine in a library, but in fact the semi-compiled form is often bulkier than the source form. The real virtues of separating the compiling and linkage stages are (*a*) that it permits

5

the compiling of very large programs, and (*b*) that the semi-compiled form provides a convenient common interface when it is desired to mix sections of programs written in different languages. (It should be made clear that we are not querying the practice of dividing a program up into semi-independent modules: the only question being discussed is whether to compile piecemeal or en masse.)

2 User's view

This chapter gives a brief account of the user's view of assemblers and describes the sort of features that are provided in a typical assembler. No effort is made to describe any particular assembly language in detail; for this, reference should be made to manufacturers' literature. The aim is to give examples of facilities which occur typically and which are of interest to the implementer.

2.1 Symbolic instructions

An instruction usually consists of an operation code (henceforth abbreviated to *opcode*) and an 'address' field that may be divided into a number of subfields, depending on the hardware of the machine Examples are:

```
LAC BASE
ADN 7 ALPHA
121 127 0 (90)
```

The opcode is usually a symbol, though it may sometimes be an octal or hexadecimal integer. Each subfield in the address can be a symbol or an *expression* in which the operands are symbols and integers, and the operators include addition, subtraction, and sometimes multiplication, division and logical operations. (Ideally, an address field should be permitted an arbitrary degree of complexity, but restrictions are very often imposed; for example, the System 360 Assembler[1] limits the number of symbols that can appear in an address to three.) A special symbol is often provided to signify the address of the register into which the current instruction will be loaded; asterisk is a common choice. This is of use in relative jumps, for example TRA * + 2 would skip one instruction.

2.2 Labels

All assemblers allow a *label* to be attached to an instruction or a data item, so that it can be referred to symbolically from elsewhere in the program. The label is a symbol, and attaching it to an item is an implicit definition of the symbol, which takes as its value the address into which that item will be loaded.* How the label is attached to an item depends on the instruction format, in a way that will now be described.

2.3 Fixed and free format instructions

An instruction can be regarded as made up of a number of *fields*; the simplest form would be two fields, opcode and address. To this can be added a *label*, and possibly a descriptive *comment*. In a fixed format scheme the various fields are recognised by their position on the line; this is most natural when the input medium is the punched card. In such a scheme, fields might be allocated as follows:

Columns	Field
1 to 6	Label (may be empty)
10 to 15	Opcode
20 to 49	Address
50 to 72	Comment (may be empty)
73 to 80	Ignored by assembler

For input from paper tape or from a remote console, fixed format is only practicable if the keyboard is fitted with a tab mechanism. In the absence of such a facility, a free format is generally adopted, in which the fields are separated by *delimiters*. A typical scheme would be as follows:

   (i) Label field terminated by a comma.
  (ii) Opcode terminated by a blank.
 (iii) Address terminated by end of line or by reverse slash, in which case the remainder of the line is comment.

* Or more precisely, the address which that item will occupy when the program is obeyed. This is usually the same as the load address, but may not be.

8

There are many variants on these schemes. A common one is a semifixed format in which the label occupies a fixed field, the opcode starts in a fixed position, but is terminated by a blank, the address starting at the first non-blank column after the opcode. This can be extended to permit a blank to terminate the address field, the rest of the line being regarded as comment.

2.4 Literals

It is often convenient for the programmer to be able to write the actual operand in the address field of an instruction. To distinguish this from an ordinary address, the operand is preceded by a warning marker, for example

LDA = 3.14159

(In the case of a decimal literal, context suffices to identify it, but the warning marker is almost universally called for.) Presented with this, the assembler stores the constant and fills in the address appropriately, thus the effect is as if the programmer had written LDA CONST, and arranged for the constant 3.14159 to be stored in a register labelled CONST. Most assemblers are smart enough to recognise repetition of literal operands, and only to store one copy of each distinct operand.

Some assemblers go further. For example, on the PDP7 a literal operand is enclosed in brackets, and can be anything that will generate a binary word. Thus

LAC (LAC TEMP)

would at run-time load into the accumulator the binary representation of the order LAC TEMP. This facilitates using the CPU to modify instructions, which is necessary on a machine such as the PDP7 that does not have any index registers. Some machines include a set of arithmetic orders for which the operand is written in the address field (so-called immediate addressing); for example, on the ICL 1900 series, ADX 0 N will add the contents of register N to accumulator zero, whereas ADN 0 N will add *the integer* N to accumulator zero. A really smart assembler would recognise the situation in which a hardware literal address can be used, and adjust

9

the opcode accordingly, replacing **ADX 0 = N** by **ADN 0 N.** Very few assemblers, however, would recognise this situation.

2.5 Directives and pseudo-operations

A typical piece of program will include, in addition to symbolic instructions and data, items commonly called *directives*, which do not cause anything to be directly assembled into the object program, but control the way in which the assembler operates. One such directive is the equivalence operation, which defines a new symbol to have the same value as an existing symbol. A common way of writing this is

ALPHA   EQU   BETA

It will be observed that the symbol being defined occurs in the label field, the defining symbol occurs in the address field, whilst the operation field contains the directive EQU. A thing such as EQU is called a *pseudo-operation*, because it occurs in the opcode field. An alternative approach, used in free format systems, is to precede a directive by a special character, for example:

DEFINE   ALPHA,   BETA

The other pseudo-operation (directive) that occurs in all assemblers is END, which signifies the end of a routine or program.

Related to the EQU operation is the pseudo-operation SET. In use it appears in the form

symbol   SET   expression

which has the effect of evaluating the expression and then defining the symbol with this value. It is usual to require that the expression shall not include any undefined symbols, though this is not strictly necessary. It is important to appreciate the difference between SET and EQU. If we write **A EQU B**, the effect of this is that in future, whenever A occurs it is as if B had been written in its place; consequently, any change in the value of B is effectively a change in the value of A also. If on the other hand we write **A SET B**, this defines A to have the same value as B, but any subsequent change in the value of B will not affect the value of A. (Compare 'call-by-name' and 'call-by-value' in ALGOL.) In practice, SET is used to attach a symbolic name to a commonly used numerical value, whilst EQU is used when two pieces of program have been written using different names for the same thing. (Note that not all assemblers make this distinction between SET and EQU; indeed, some use EQU with the meaning here ascribed to SET.)

2.6 Origin setting

Most assemblers have a pseudo operation to set the location counter and so determine where the next item of code will be placed. Typically this will be called ORG, and for example

ORG * + 16

will advance the location counter by 16 (leaving 16 words unused). The origin must necessarily be relative to the start of the routine, since at assembly time its position in core is not known. Some assemblers provide also another pseudo-operation, AORG, which sets the location counter to an absolute address. This is contrary to the spirit of independent assembly of routines, and is not usual.

2.7 Data-generating pseudo-operations

The concept of a pseudo-operation can be extended to include the generation of data words. Typical operations are DECIMAL and OCTAL; these occur in the operation field, with the 'address' field containing one or more constants of appropriate type. If a label is attached, it will correspond to the first data word generated. Thus

TABLE   DECIMAL   3.4, 4.3, 2.89, 445.789

would generate four data words, the first being labelled TABLE.

An alternative approach which is convenient when there are many different types of constant is to have a single pseudo-operation and to preface each constant with a code letter indicating its type. For example, using I, F and O to indicate fixed-point, floating-point and octal constants respectively, we might have pseudo-operation DC (define constants) used as follows:

TABLE   DC   I34, I102, F3.14159, O17777, I3

11

The assembler incorporated in the IBM OS/360[1] allows each constant to be prefaced by a repetition count, for example

LIST   DC   8I3

would generate eight fixed-point constants, all with value 3. The parallel with FORTRAN format statements is obvious.

2.8 Storage allocation

Pseudo-operations are provided to reserve areas of store; these can take various forms. Typically, two might be provided, BSS and BES
The line of code

SYMB   BSS n

reserves a block of n registers, with the symbol SYMB defined as the address of the *first* word, whilst

SYMB   BES n

reserves n registers with SYMB defined as the address of the *last* word of the block.*

It is often the case that data items of different types take up differing amounts of storage space. For example, on a short word-length machine a floating-point number will occupy two or more words. In such a situation it may be inconvenient to tot up the amount of store that must be reserved, and a pseudo-operation can be designed to help. Such a psuedo-operation might be called DS (define storage), and would be used as follows:

SYMB   DS   3F,5I

will reserve space for three floating-point numbers and five fixed-point numbers. There is an obvious analogy with DC. (This version of DS is a simplified form of the facility provided in OS/360.)

Another aspect of storage allocation is the allocation of space to data items that appear as symbolic names in the program. One approach is to require that all data names be declared at the start

* The motivation for this can be found in the fact that some machines, notably the IBM 709x, *subtract* the contents of the index register from the address when modification takes place. There is then an attraction in storing arrays backwards.

of a routine, storage being allocated there and then. At the other extreme is the convention that the use of a symbol as a data name implicitly allocates storage for that item of data. Both schemes have disadvantages. The first is tedious for the programmer, but provides protection against misspelling (since a misspelt name will appear to be use of an undeclared name). The second is convenient to the programmer, but provides no error-check. A compromise sometimes encountered (e.g. in the PDP7 Assembler[2]) is to provide automatic allocation for any symbol which is preceded by a special character; storage is allocated at the end of the program without further action by the programmer. This is very convenient for temporary (scratch) storage.

2.9 Scope of symbols

When routines are separately assembled, the question of the scope of definition of the symbols arises. Usually two scopes are recognised, *local* symbols, which have a meaning only in the routine in which they are defined, and *global* symbols which have a meaning in all routines. (See Chapter 5 for elaborations on this theme.) The usual convention is that symbols are local unless otherwise stated; global symbols can be defined either by a special marker or by a pseudo-operation. Thus one might write:

```
*AREL2  LDA  BASE
```

the asterisk signifying a global definition; or on the alternative convention:

```
AREL2  ENTRY
       LDA     BASE
```

the pseudo-operation ENTRY defining this label as a globally valid entry point. Note that on this second convention we could write:

```
AREL2  ENTRY
BGIN   LDA    BASE
```

in which case the symbols AREL2 and BGIN would both refer to the same instruction. However, BGIN could only be used within the routine, whereas AREL2 could be used inside or outside the routine.

13

From an efficiency point of view, references to global labels are more 'expensive' than references to local labels, so that it is good practice to use double labelling for points that must be referred to both inside and outside a routine. In addition to defining global symbols, a routine may refer to global symbols defined in other routines. These may be recognised by applying the rule 'any symbol used that is not local must be global'; alternatively, the assembler may require that all such symbols must be specified using a pseudo-operation EXTERNAL.

The above discussion has been mainly concerned with reference to program labels in other routines. Some assemblers allow references to data items in other routines in a similar way. More commonly, however, global data is placed in COMMON areas (as in FORTRAN), and a routine referencing such areas will include COMMON declarations at its head.

2.10 Disguising the order code

The assembler can often hide from the programmer peculiarities of the order structure. For example, on the PDP7 one operation code is used for a whole family of input/output operations; since these do not require an operand from store, the 'address' digits are used to distinguish the various operations. The assembler allows the programmer to use a different operation code for each I/O operation, and generates the appropriate address digits.

2.11 Symbols representing instructions

In the PDP7 assembly language a symbol stands for an 18-bit quantity (the PDP7 has a word length of 18 bits). Normally, a symbol stands for an opcode or address, and is appropriately filled out with zeros to make up the 18 bits, but if desired a symbol can stand for a full 18-bit instruction. For example, suppose there is a subroutine called RDKB to read characters from the teletype keyboard; this would be called by the instruction JMS RDKB. The programmer can define a symbol READ by the directive

READ = JMS RDKB

and thereafter can write the single word **READ** instead of the sub-routine call. Judicious use of this facility can greatly increase the readability of a program.

2.12 Conditional assembly

This facility makes it possible to determine whether or not something shall be included in the assembly on the basis of a relation between symbols. It is particularly useful when a program has to cope with a variety of environmental circumstances and it is desired to include only those sections appropriate to the current situation. In its simplest form the facility is controlled by two pseudo-operations, **IFF** (if-false) and **IFT** (if-true). These differ only in the sense of the test; strictly speaking, only one of the pair is necessary. **IFT** is used as follows:

IFT   symbol-1   relation   symbol-2

causes the following line of code to be included in the assembly only if the condition (symbol-1 relation symbol-2) is true. The relation can be .EQ. (equals), .NE. (not equals), .GT. (greater than), etc.

More elaborate conditional assembly facilities can be obtained by making use of assembly-time jumps and labels. Typically, assembly-time labels (or *sequence symbols*) are preceded by a period and appear in the label field. However, they are ignored by the assembler except in the context of two new pseudo-instructions **AGO** and **AIF**. Let **.SS** be sequence symbol, then

AGO   .SS

causes assembly to be continued from the line in which the symbol .SS appears in the label field. (Usually, this must be a forward jump.)

AIF   (symbol-1   relation   symbol-2)   .SS

causes assembly to be continued from the line labelled .SS if the condition is true; otherwise assembly continues with the next line of code, as usual. This allows one of two blocks of code to be assembled, as follows:

15

```
        AIF    (X .EQ. Y)  .SS1
            block 1
        AGO  .SS2
.SS1
            block 2
.SS2
```

If X and Y have the same value block 2 is included, otherwise block 1 is included.

2.13 Default setting of symbols

This form of conditional assembly appears to have been provided only in the ABL assembler for ATLAS 1,[3] an assembler that had otherwise very little to commend it. It allows the programmer to specify a value to be taken by a symbol if, by the end of assembly, no other definition has been encountered. It was widely used in Atlas library routines to give standard options that could easily be overridden by the user.

2.14 Addressing mechanisms

The IBM System/360 is typical of a class of machines that use a 'two-dimensional' addressing mechanism. The address field of an instruction specifies a register that holds a base address, and a displacement to be added to that address. Whilst this system of addressing is often useful for data areas, for program addresses one does not want to be bothered with explicit base registers, and so the assembler must take a symbolic address and break it up into a base-displacement pair. In order that the assembler can interpret such addresses, the programmer must indicate which registers are being used as base registers, and what their contents will be at run time. (He must necessarily indicate this in symbolic form, since absolute addresses are not assigned until load time.) This is done in the S/360 by a pseudo operation, USING.
Thus

        USING   FRED, 3

16

indicates that register 3 is being used as a base register, and that its contents at run time will be the address corresponding to the symbolic address FRED. More common in S/360 in the following usage:

```
BALR   3,0
USING  *,3
```

BALR 3,0 loads into register 3 the address of the next introduction, and USING *,3 indicates that register 3 can be used as a base register and contains the current instruction address. This pair will frequently be found at the start of a routine.

2.15 Repetitive assembly

It is often convenient to be able to generate sequences of code that are basically identical, differing in some particular in a systematic manner; this need arises, for example, when constructing tables. It can be achieved by a repetition pseudo-operation **DUP**, as follows:

DUP n,m causes the following n lines of code to be repeated in the assembly m times. Moreover, there is a special character, $ say, which is replaced by 1 in the first occurrence of the block, 2 in the second occurrence, and so on up to m in the last repetition. For example:

```
DUP   2,5
LAC   BASE + $
STO   TABLE + $
```

would generate

```
LAC   BASE + 1
STO   TABLE + 1
LAC   BASE + 2
STO   TABLE + 2
LAC   BASE + 3
STO   TABLE + 3
LAC   BASE + 4
STO   TABLE + 4
LAC   BASE + 5
STO   TABLE + 5
```

2.16 Multiple location counters

Some assemblers allow program to be assembled with respect to two or more location counters, so that pieces of code that will be disjoint in the final program may be interspersed in the source form. This facility is useful in systems where it is necessary to keep a close control on the exact position in store into which sections of program are placed, but on the whole the modern trend is towards leaving that sort of decision to the assembly system. Exceptions occur, even so; for example, it might be necessary in a certain computer for I/O channel commands to be placed in particular registers in the store. It is convenient for the programmer to write the channel commands at the points where they naturally occur amongst the rest of the code, and this can be achieved with two location counters, as follows:

```
A    ORG  100     set location counter A
B    ORG  17777   set location counter B
     USE  A
        program
     USE  B
        channel commands
     USE  A
        program
     USE  B
        channel commands
     USE  A
        etc.
```

The channel commands will go into consecutive registers from 17777 upwards, whilst the program occupies consecutive registers from 100 upwards.

In the above example, multiple location counters were just a convenience. Sometimes the machine architecture forces their use. For example, in the ICL 1900 series only the first 4096 words of store can be directly addressed for data fetches: for the remainder of the store a modified address must be used. The store allocation to a program is therefore made in three regions:

	LOWER	for data directly addressed
	PROGRAM	for instructions
and	UPPER	for the remainder of the data.

The assembler keeps three location counters so that reference to these areas can be intermingled, as in the following example.

# PROGRAM	sets PROGRAM location counter
CALL 7 PRLCT	
# LOWER	sets LOWER location counter and allocates two registers
CTNWP, CTLSP	
# PROGRAM	resets PROGRAM location counter.
LDX 0 CTN	
STO 0 CTNWP	

Multiple location counters may also appear implicitly: for example, when literal operands are used these are often stored in an area of store addressed by a separate location counter.

2.17 Overlays

The technique of overlaying involves holding parts of a program on some external storage device (disc or tape) and bringing them into core as required. Thus the same area of core may be occupied at different times by different pieces of program. All the complication comes in the linkage editor and loader (and is discussed in Chapter 5). The assembler must provide pseudo-operations by which the programmer can indicate how the program is divided up; that is, which sections may be in core simultaneously, and which sections will occupy the same area of store at different times. He must also be able to specify which symbolic data addresses are common to all overlays, so that storage for these can be assigned in an area that will not be overwritten. All this information is passed on by the assembler to the linkage editor and loader.

```
0000   #STEER        LIST
       00000000      20/03/69    COMPILED BY XPLG 26A

0001   #PROGRAM      CTMT70/SEGA                              CTM0010
0002   #LOWER                                                 CTM0020
0003   #LOWER        BUFFA(1002)                              CTM0030
0004   RCRD          3/0,0,8Q,0/BUFFA                         CTM0050
0005

0006   PARER         24%INCORRECT PARAMETER CARD              CTM0060

0007   MESS          24/PARER                                 CTM0070
0008   MASK          #60077777                                CTM0080
0009   CRDBL         25                                       CTM0090
0010   BLKSZ         501                                      CTM0110
0011   TAPE          261/#400,0,0,0,0,0,0,0,0,0,0,0,0         CTM0110

0012                 0,0,0,0,0,0,0,0,0,0,0,0,0                CTM0120

0013   #PROGRAM                                               CTM0130
0014   #ENTRY                                                 CTM0140
0015   START  ALLOT    0        [ALLOT CARD READER            CTM0150
0016          LDX      CRO                                    CTM0160
0017          BPZ  0   9        [TEST FOR ALLOCATION          CTM0170
0018          SUSWT    *+3      [NO CARD READER AVAILABLE      CTM0180
0019          BN   0   2NCR                                   CTM0200
0020          PERI     RCRT     [READ PARAMETER CARD          CTM0210
0021          SUSBY 0  3
```

```
                                           LV
                                           LP

0    #00300000
1    #00000020
2    #00000120
3    #51564357
4    #62624543
5    #64206041
6    #62455225
7    #64455224
8    #43416264
9    #53000004
10   #03000000
11   #60077777
12   #00000031
13   #00000765
14   #00000000
15   #00000000
16   #00000000
17   #00000000
18   #00000000
19   #00000000
20   #00000000
21   #00000000
22   #00000000
23   #00000000
24   #00000000
25   #00000000
26   #00000000
27   #00000000
28   #00000000
29   #00000000
30   #00000000
31   #00000000
32   #00000000
33   #00000000
34   #00000000
35   #00000000
36   #00000000
37   #00000000
38   #00000000
39   #00000000
40   #00000000
41   #00000000
42   #00000000
43   #00000000

0    156  0  0       3P
1    100  0  0
2    054  0  0  2290 5 PR
3    161  0  0       3P
4    064  0  0
5    074  0  0       PR
6    150  0  0       3P
```

Fig. 2.1. Example of assembler listing (reproduced by permission of International Computers Ltd)

2.18 Listings

An assembler provides a variety of information about the program that it has assembled. Besides details of any obvious errors—incorrect syntax, multiple definition of symbols, etc.—the following may be provided:

(i) Listing of symbolic instructions side by side with generated binary or binary-symbolic code.

(ii) Table of symbols defined in a routine, with or without their values.

(iii) Table of symbols used in a routine.

(iv) Cross-reference table: for each symbol defined, its name, value and a list of all the instructions that reference it.

The form of listing is usually controlled by one or more pseudo-operations, for example:

LIST FULL
LIST NONE
LIST SYMBOLS
etc.

Another common pseudo-operation is EJECT, which causes a page feed on the printer at this point in the listing.

An example of the listing from the ICL PLAN assembler is given in Fig. 2.1. The source lines are printed alongside the generated code. Each item of generated code is preceded by its address, in the form of a location counter and a displacement relative to that location counter. If the item is an instruction, the address is printed on a relative address followed by the appropriate location counter.

3 Symbol tables

Most of the work of an assembler is concerned with converting symbolic representations of computer words into binary form, and this conversion is based on one or more *symbol tables*. A symbol table consists of a number of *entries*, each of which associates a *symbol* with a *value*. There are two distinct problems to be considered: the mechanistic one of how to organise the table so that new entries can be made and existing entries consulted, and the semantic one of what to associate with a symbol as its value. For example, if a symbol stands for an operation code, its value is the binary pattern representing the operation in machine code. But suppose that a symbol stands for a storage register whose address is as yet unknown; then this information must be recorded in the symbol table, and is regarded as the value of the symbol.

This chapter deals with the organisation of the symbol table; the semantic problem of defining values is left to later chapters. As a start, let us consider a very simple symbol table which contains only operation codes. This has two important characteristics. First the number of entries is constant and known in advance, and second, since operation codes are usually restricted to three or four letters the symbol can conveniently be represented in the table by one word containing the symbol in character form. (For example, on a 24-bit machine using 6-bit characters, four characters can be packed in one word.)

Symbols that have fewer than the maximum number of characters are filled out on the right by blanks. A section of the table is shown in Fig. 3.1.

Given a symbol, we require to find its value from the table. The simplest strategy is the *linear search*, in which each entry is examined in turn until a coincidence is established. It is readily seen that if the table contains N entries, and if all symbols occur with equal frequency, then on average $N/2$ entries will be examined for each symbol whose value is required. In practice, of course, symbols do not occur with equal frequency—the operation code 'STOP', for example, does not occur frequently—and if a linear search is employed the table should be ordered so that the most frequently

A D X b	100000
A D N b	100001
C A L L	101100

Fig. 3.1. Section of symbol table
(b *indicates blank*)

required entries occur near the beginning. It is, however, impossible to achieve optimum ordering, and it is therefore worth examining alternative strategies. Two important methods are the *logarithmic search,* and *alphabetic indexing.*

The Logarithmic Search. The word containing the characters of the symbol can be regarded as a binary integer, and the table ordered so that these words occur in increasing numerical order. To locate an arbitrary symbol in the table we make a numerical comparison of this symbol with the symbol halfway through the table. This immediately determines whether the wanted symbol is in the first or second half of the table. Repeating the process in the appropriate half of the table will locate the symbol within a quarter of the table, a further comparison will locate it within an eighth of the table, and so on. This process, also known as the 'binary chop', is very efficient; it requires of order $\log_2 N$ comparisons to locate an arbitrary symbol. The following table shows the benefit of the method:

N	Linear search $(N/2)$	Log search $(\log_2 N)$
32	16	5
1024	512	10
32768	16384	15

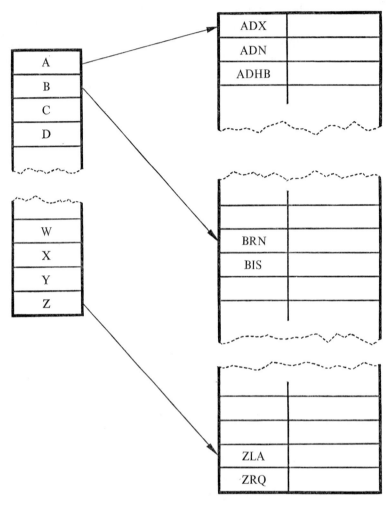

Fig. 3.2. Section of symbol table using alphabetic indexing

Alphabetic Indexing. This method presupposes that the symbols are arranged in alphabetic order of the leftmost character. An auxiliary table is constructed which points to the start of each sub-section in the main table, as shown in Fig. 3.2.

In effect, the main table has been replaced by 26 subtables, and the auxiliary table indexes the start of the subtables. It should be noted that, once the appropriate subtable has been determined from the initial letter. it can be searched in a number of ways. Usually it will be short enough for a linear search to be reasonable, but a logarithmic search, or even another stage of alphabetic indexing, could be employed.

3.1 Hash tables

The symbol table considered so far is characterised by the fact that it contains a fixed number of entries, which is known before the table is constructed. This is not true of a table which deals with programmer-defined symbols. These are not known in advance, and the table has to be built up dynamically: the typical operation is, given a symbol, to determine whether or not it is in the table, and if not, add it to the table. This effectively precludes any table look-up method that depends on some special ordering of the symbols, since inserting a new symbol whilst retaining the ordering is a very expensive operation. A solution is found in the *hash table* (variously known also as the scatter table, random table, computed-entry table, or key transformation table). The hash table is an example of a programming technique that was independently discovered by a number of people, and extensively used before it achieved the dignity of a formal name. A comprehensive survey, which references all the earlier papers on the subject, is given by Morris.[4]

The hash table achieves a subdivision of a large table into subtables that are small enough to be searched using a linear search, without requiring any particular ordering of the items. Suppose that the table contains N items. A simple hash technique is to divide these entries into 10 groups, the ith group having n_i entries, where $n_i \sim N/10$. This is achieved by a *hashing function* which generates from each symbol an integer in the range 0 to 9, with the property that all values are generated with roughly equal probability in a fairly random way. Another way of putting this is to say that the hashing function allocates each symbol to one of 10 groups in a random manner. For example, if the symbol is stored in a single computer word as a sequence of packed characters, regarding it as an

25

integer and dividing by 10 will give a remainder which lies in the range 0 to 9; this can be used as the hash code to allocate the symbol to one of ten groups. In this form the hash table technique is often known as the *bucket sort*. Because of the random nature of the hashing function, the groups will not all be of the same size. A common technique is to store the symbols on a number of chained lists, the hashing function being used to select one of the lists, and a new symbol being placed in a free cell and chained onto the appropriate list. A symbol table organised on these lines is described by Braden and Wulf[5].

The idea of a hash table can be extended into a form particularly suitable for an assembler, and it is this form that we now describe. We consider a situation in which each entry in the table consists of two items, a symbol and its associated value, and the maximum number of entries to be accommodated is N. (This is not restrictive; we shall see later how the table can be extended automatically if need be.) The table is initially set up with room for m entries, where m is of order $3N/2$, and each entry is marked in some convenient way as 'empty'. A hashing function is devised which will produce from each symbol an integer in the range 0 to $m - 1$. This can be done by dividing the symbol, regarded as an integer, by m and taking the remainder. A variant is to multiply the integer form of the symbol by some constant, and then divide the result by m. Alternatively, if m is a power of 2, it suffices to take certain of the characters of the symbol and concatenate their binary representations. For example, with a 6-bit character code, concatenation of the first and last characters gives a 12-bit integer, and the middle six bits then give a hash value between 0 and 63. For a detailed discussion of hash coding the reader should consult the paper by Morris already referred to.

Suppose the contents of the jth entry in the table is denoted by $T(j)$, then the procedure for entering a new item is as follows. Let h be the hash value computed from the symbol by the hash function. The entry $T(h)$ is examined; if this is marked 'empty' the new item is entered here, otherwise h is replaced by $h + 1$ mod m, and this new entry examined, continuing in this way until an empty entry is found, at which point the item is inserted.

In the form described this technique is very dependent on the randomness of the hashing function, since if the function tends to produce values unevenly spread over the range 0 to $m - 1$ clustering of items will occur in the table, with consequent slowing of table look-up. To avoid clustering a quadratic search can be used, so that if the entry $T(h)$ is occupied the successive addresses searched are $(h + i^2)[\text{mod } m]$ for $i = 1, 2, \ldots, (m - 1)/2$. For this method to work m must be a prime number. A disadvantage is that only $(m - 1)/2$ entries are searched, but Day[6] has described a variant in which all entries are searched if m is a prime of the form $4n + 3$.

To look up an item in the table the procedure is similar. The hash function is applied to the symbol, yielding h, and $T(h)$ is examined. If this entry is empty, the symbol is not in the table; otherwise, let $T(h)$ be the pair S, V. If S is identical with the symbol being looked up, V is the associated value, otherwise replace h by $h + 1$ mod m and examine this entry, continuing until a coincidence is found or an empty entry is encountered, this latter contingency indicating that the desired symbol is not in the table. A common requirement in an assembler is to build up a table which contains one entry for each distinct symbol occurring in the program. This is readily done by extending the above algorithm, so that if the symbol is not found in the table (as evinced by encountering an empty entry), it is inserted in that empty entry.

It will be seen that this technique is well adapted to a table of dynamically varying size. The efficiency of the process is measured by the number of entries that have to be examined to locate a particular symbol, which obviously depends on the density of symbols in the table. If the table is only sparsely filled, the symbol required will usually be located in one go. As the table fills up, the chance that more than one symbol contained will have the same hash value increases, and the likelihood of having to examine several entries goes up. The exact performance depends on the choice of the hash function as well as the size of the table. Peterson[7] carried out simulations to determine the average number of entries examined in order to locate an arbitrary symbol. and Schay and Spruth[8] derived a formula for the same purpose. Their results are summarised in Table 1.

From Table 1 it is apparent that the performance deteriorates rapidly when the table is nearly full. In this situation, the remedy is to set up a larger table, and to re-enter the items in the new table. This can be done automatically if a suitable criterion can be devised for deciding when to extend the table. Essentially, one has to balance the time taken in constructing the new table against the time saved by the improved performance of the larger, and hence emptier,

λ	p (*Simulation*)	p (*Formula*)
0·2	1·137	1·125
0·4	1·366	1·335
0·6	1·823	1·750
0·8	3·223	3·000
1	16·914	(not applicable)

Table 1. Hash table performance. [λ *is the ratio* (*number of occupied entries*)/(*total number of entries*). p *is the average number of entries examined to locate an arbitrary symbol.*]

table. Obviously, this involves some hypothesising about the number of times the table is going to be consulted in the future. Hopgood[9] has investigated this problem and shows that if each entry will be accessed once more it is not worth extending until the table is 80% full, whereas if each entry will be accessed six times it is worth extending the table when it is 40% full.

We have assumed so far that the symbols are actually stored in the table. This implies a restriction in length to something like four or six characters. This is an irksome restriction for the programmer (though unfortunately a common one), and it can easily be removed. The following technique is one of many ways; it is based on a technique devised for the CPL compiler[10], and has much in common with a method described by Mealy[11] in a classic paper on assembly techniques. The essence of the method is that the external form of the symbol—the *print name*—is stored in a dictionary, and that for all other purposes the symbol is replaced by an integer that defines its position in the dictionary. To allow completely arbitrary length of symbols, there is associated with the dictionary an auxiliary *dictionary look-up* table DLU; the jth entry in this, DLU(j), gives the position in the dictionary of the start of the jth symbol, and the number of characters comprising that symbol, nj.

The procedure for entering a new symbol in the table is as follows: Let X_i denote the symbol. The next free place in the dictionary is found, and the symbol is entered, the DLU table being updated also. Let x_i be the position in DLU of the entry pertaining to X_i.

The next step is to apply the hash function to X_i. Since the ultimate size of the table is unknown, it is convenient to use a hash function with a range that bears no relation to the size of the table, m, and to take its result mod m. Having found a random entry in this way. the procedure is to enter, in the first free entry found starting from the selected one, the *three* quantities $H(X_i)$, x_i, and the value (where $H(X_i)$ denotes the value of the hash function *before* it was reduced modulo m).

To look up a symbol in the table, the procedure is first to compute the hash value $H(X)$, and to examine the entry $H(X)$ mod m. If this is empty, the symbol is not in the table. If not, let the three quantities entered there be H, x and V. Test if $H = H(X)$: if not, we know that this is not the symbol being looked for. If $H = H(X)$, use x to index the DLU, and compare the length recorded in the DLU with the length of the symbol under consideration; if they do not agree this entry can be discarded. If they do agree, it is necessary to get the full form of the symbol from the dictionary and compare character by character to see if it agrees with the symbol under consideration. If there is an exact coincidence the symbol has been found and V is the value. If any of these tests fail, we examine the next entry $(H(X)$ mod $m + 1)$ mod m, and proceed until either a coincidence is found or an empty entry is encountered. It will be seen that this technique avoids doing any character-by-character comparisons unless absolutely necessary. As before, setting up the table and looking up can be combined; if a symbol is not in the table an attempt to look it up will lead to an empty entry, and the symbol can then be inserted.

Extension of the table when it becomes full is achieved by setting up a larger table of size m', and entering the triple $\{H(X_i), x_i, \text{value}\}$ in the first free position found starting at $H(x_i)$ mod m'. This is achieved without reference to the dictionary, or the DLU table.

This concludes our discussion of the mechanics of symbol tables. In the chapters that follow, it will be assumed that symbol tables can be constructed and interrogated, and attention will be concentrated on the information to be stored in them.

4 Two-pass assemblers

The two-pass assembler can be described as the 'classic' assembler. It exists on most machines, varying in detail, but the same in fundamental design.

4.1 Strategy

The assembler takes a *routine* (or subprogram) and converts it into binary symbolic form for subsequent processing by a linkage editor. The basic strategy is very simple. The first pass through the source program collects all the symbol definitions into a symbol table, and the second pass converts the program to binary symbolic form, using the definitions collected in the first pass. (The merit of a separate pass to collect symbol definitions is that it obviates the tricky situation which arises if an occurrence of a symbol has to be processed before the symbol has been defined—see Chapter 6 for more on this point.) Although the program is scanned twice, only in the crudest systems is the physical source material read twice. If the assembler is reading directly from cards, then the source material can be copied on to magnetic tape or disc during the first pass, and so preserved for the second pass. In the environment of an operating system, it is likely that the assembler will in any case read card images from tape or disc, so that the problem does not arise,

4.2 Rules for classifying symbolic expressions

During the second pass, the assembler will have to recognise three sorts of quantities: absolute quantities, relocatable quantities and references to externally defined symbols. In the simplest case all relocatable quantities are expressed relative to an origin at the beginning of the routine. The assembler therefore has to categorise expressions that appear in the various fields of an instruction, and does this by assigning a *mode*, which can be *absolute, relocatable* or *undetermined*. The mode of an expression is determined by the following rules:

   (i) An expression which contains external symbols is of undetermined mode (but see below).

   (ii) An expression in absolute mode is either a constant, a symbol with an absolute value, the *difference* between two symbols which have relative values, or any combination of these constituents.

   (iii) An expression in relocatable mode consists either of a single symbol which has a relative value, or one such symbol to which is added an expression of absolute mode (which may be negative).

Note that the sum or product of two symbols whose values are relative, or the product of a relative and an absolute symbol, is meaningless, and that expressions containing such combinations are classified as malformed.

If addition and subtraction are the only arithmetic operations allowed in expressions, the mode of an expression is readily determinded. If the expression does not contain any external symbols, we replace relative symbols by 1, absolute symbols and constants by 0, and evaluate the resulting expression. This determines the mode as follows:

$$< 0 \text{ malformed}$$
$$0 \text{ absolute}$$
$$1 \text{ relocatable}$$
$$\geqslant 2 \text{ malformed}$$

If the expression contains external symbols, it can be divided into two subexpressions, one containing only external symbols, and one containing no external symbols. The mode is undetermined, but it will generally be useful to evaluate the mode of the nonexternal expression, so that when the external symbols are eventually defined the mode of the complete expression can be found (and checked, to make sure it is not malformed).

If multiplication is allowed in expressions, the rules for determining the mode must be extended. Consider first an expression without

31

external symbols. Then any product can only involve constants and absolute symbols, since multiplication of relative quantities is meaningless. So in this case the rules are:

(i) If a relative symbol appears as one of the operands of a multiplication operation, the expression is malformed.

(ii) Otherwise, replace relative symbols by 1, absolute symbols and constants by zero, and evaluate as before.

If external symbols occur in the expression the mode is undetermined, but it may be desirable to determine the mode as far as possible. To achieve this, we first observe that any valid expression can be arranged in the following canonical form:

$$R + A \pm S_1 \pm S_2 \pm S_3 \ldots \pm P_1 \pm P_2 \ldots \pm P_n$$

Here R is a relocatable symbol, A is an absolute expression, S_i are external symbols and P_i are products including external symbols (since any other product will be subsumed in A). The partial mode is then determined from R and A in a straightforward manner.

These rules require amendment if more than one location counter is in use, since there will now be several origins for relocatable quantities. If we impose the restriction that two relative symbols related to different location counters may not appear in the same expression, then the rules as given above can still be applied.

4.3 The output from the assembler

The exact form of the output depends on the linkage editor. Typically, the assembler might produce the following output:

Header	Name of routine
RLB	Relocatable binary section: consists of binary-symbolic code and relocation information
Definition table	Definitions of global symbols defined in the routine
Use table	Details of use of global symbols in the routine

The definition table carries information about symbols defined in this routine which are to have a global meaning. Since these may be absolute or relative, the table must carry this information as well as the value. In the case of a relative symbol the value is relative to the beginning of the routine.

The use table is more complex, since it records all occurrences of global symbols within the routine. Its exact form will depend on the facilities provided by the assembler, in particular the circumstances in which global symbols can be used. It will be seen later that if multiplication of global symbols is allowed an additional table, the *product use table* is also required.

If multiple location counters are used, an extra block must be output giving the amount of space used by the routine relative to each location counter. Each relocatable item will carry with it an indication of the relevant location counter.

4.4 Cross-reference and the use table

The simplest form of cross-referencing occurs when the only external references are calls to other routines, all references to global data being channelled through a COMMON area, as in FOR-TRAN[12, 13].

References to COMMON data are dealt with by introducing another location counter, and the only cross references to be dealt with are those that occur in jump or subroutine call instructions. There are two basic methods which both depend on the fact that the external symbol will be the only component of the address of the instruction in question. The first option is for the use table to record for each external symbol the places in the routine where it has been used. Then, when the value of the symbol is eventually determined, there is sufficient information for the linkage editor to insert the value in the right places. An elegant variation is to use the vacant address fields to chain together all references to a given external symbol, the head of the chain being held in the use table.

The second option is to make use of a *transfer vector*. This vector comprises a set of registers immediately preceding the first instruction of the routine. In a machine with indirect addressing, any reference to an external symbol is converted into an indirect reference to the relevant register of the transfer vector. For example, using an asterisk to indicate indirect addressing:

```
TRA  JOE                         L1  NOP  0
............                     L2  NOP  0
TRA  FRED    generates the           TRA * L1
............    equivalent of        .........
TRA  JOE                             TRA * L2
                                     .........
                                     TRA * L1
```

The use table is simple, since there is by definition only one place in each routine where the external symbol is needed. Indeed, if symbols are restricted to a small number of characters the use table can be combined with the transfer vector, making use of the fact that the address field of the transfer vector entry is spare. Thus the example given above would become:

```
L1  NOP  'JOE'
L2  NOP  'FRED'
    .........
    TRA * L1
    .........
    TRA * L2
    .........
    TRA * L1
```

The transfer vector technique can be used without indirect addressing by making each reference to an external symbol a transfer to the corresponding transfer vector entry, and planting another transfer order in the transfer vector. This use of transfer vectors should not be confused with their use in channelling references to actual parameters in subprograms, as occurs in FORTRAN and similar systems.

If the assembler does not restrict external references to be calls of other routines, but allows arbitrary references to external data as well, the use table becomes more complicated. We first consider the situation where only addition and subtraction are allowed as operators in the address field. Then any valid address can be reduced by the assembler to the form

$$R + A \pm S_1 \pm S_2 \pm S_3 \ldots \pm S_n$$

where R is a relative (local) symbol, A is an absolute quantity, and the S_i are external symbols. The use table then has to record, for each external symbol referenced, where the reference was made and whether the external symbol is to be added or subtracted.

In the general case where multiplication is allowed, we have seen that the expression can be reduced to the form

$$R + A \pm S_1 \pm S_2 \ldots \pm S_n + P_1 \pm P_2 \ldots \pm P_m$$

As before, the S_i generate entries in the use table. We further note that since a relative symbol occurring as a component of a product makes the expression malformed, it is sufficient to consider P_i as involving at most external symbols and absolute symbols and/or constants. Since absolute symbols and constants can be multiplied immediately, we need only consider products of the form $AS_1S_2S_3 \ldots S_n$. Finally, if the P_i is preceded by a minus sign its absolute component can be complemented, so we need only consider addition of products. Such products are conveniently dealt with by introducing an auxiliary table, the *product use table*, PUT for short. (Of course, what the assembler does with a product depends on how the linkage editor is going to treat it. We are here describing only one possible strategy.) The product use table contains a number of multiword entries of varying lengths; the form of an entry is as follows:

S_1	
S_2	
...	symbols to be multiplied
...	
...	
A	absolute multiplier
adr	place where product is to be inserted

For each symbol that occurs in one or more entries in the product use table, there will be an entry in the use table with a special pointer to indicate 'used in product use table'. When a symbol is added to a

PUT entry, the use table is scanned to see if such an entry occurs for the symbol, and if not, one is created.

If other operations, such as logical operations, are allowed in addresses with external symbols as operands, when it is necessary to resort to a technique of deferred evaluation in which expressions are evaluated at linkage-edit time. This is touched on briefly on Chapter 5.

4.5 Textual processing

The input to the assembler is a string of characters. It is convenient to perform a once-for-all transformation of the input string and convert it into a sequence of basic *text items* such as symbols, constants, operators, separators etc. If this is done, the rest of the assembler does not need to concern itself with the rules for forming symbols, separating fields, etc. Moreover, the rest of the assembler becomes insensitive to differences in input code for various input media, since these can all be taken account of in the transformation. This is an obvious advantage gained from a modular structure. The structure of a typical input module is now described. It consists of two parts. The first part deals with the control of the physical input device, and produces a string of 'raw' characters in a buffer. The second part takes these raw characters and converts them into a set of text items in a simple forward scan. These can be:

> *symbols*: a symbol is a letter followed by a (possibly empty) string of alphameric characters
> *constants*: a constant is a string of decimal digits
> *operators*: +, −, *
> *separators*: blank, comma, point
> *terminators*: end-of-field (EOF), end-of-line (EOL)

When the assembler requires the next item it calls the second part of the input module; if this second part exhausts the supply of raw characters it will automatically call the first part to refill the buffer. When called, the input module returns the next item, together with a code (0, 1, 2, 3 or 4) to indicate the type of item; it can also be arranged to recognise system control cards, ignore blank cards/lines, and skip over cards containing only comment.

If the input is in fixed format the division into fields is trivial, and the above routine can be used on each field in turn. If the opcode field is terminated by blanks this is readily catered for. The first blank will be recognised as a separator, and it is then only necessary to skip to the first nonblank column to start conversion of the operation field.

A completely free format calls for a more complicated contextual analysis. Suppose that the label field, if present, is terminated by a comma, and the opcode field is terminated by a blank. The algorithm for separating the fields is then:

(i) Skip over leading blanks.
(ii) Read the next text item; this will be a symbol, which may be a label or an opcode.
(iii) Read the next text item. This will be comma or blank. If it is a comma, the symbol just read is a label, and the pointer can be advanced to the next nonblank character in preparation for reading the opcode. If it is a blank the symbol just read is the opcode; record this, and record the label field as empty, then advance the pointer to the next non-blank character in preparation for reading the address field.

Other refinements can be included. For example, the routine can recognise constructions such as .EQ., .GT., etc. as operators, and assign suitable internal representations.

The assembler has to carry out a syntactic check on the source program, and this can to a large extent be incorporated into the textual processing. This possibility arises because on most occasions when a text item is requested we have a fairly good idea what sort of text item it should be. For example, the label and opcode fields must contain symbols, and in an expression in an address field operators and operands must alternate. We can therefore define an 'expected item indicator' E as follows:

Value of E	Expecting
1	symbol
2	symbol or constant
3	operator or terminator
4	comma
5	blank or EOF
6	EOF

The input conversion routine is extended so as to take E as an input; if the item constructed does not fit the expectation as determined by the value of E a diagnostic message can be generated.* Thus the label and operand fields are extracted by the following sequence:

$E := 1$
Call TI   (Get a symbol)
$E := 5$
Call TI   (Check that there is nothing else in the field)

Whilst processing an expression in the address field, the outline sequence is:

$L:$ $E := 2$
      Call TI   *(Get operand)*
      Deal with operand
      $E := 3$
      Call TI   *(Get operator)*
      Deal with operator
      If operator $\neq$ EOF, go to L

4.6 The first pass

The purpose of the first pass has already been defined as building up a symbol table by collecting the symbol definitions. In addition it builds up the definition table whose form has already been defined. In order to carry out these operations it must process the label field to pick up symbol definitions, and it must also process the opcode field in order to pick up symbols defined by psuedo-operations. In addition it must do sufficient analysis of the program to keep track of the location counter; this involves recognising the end of an instruction, and correctly treating pseudo-operations that reserve storage, or generate data words.

---

* This technique is certainly as old as the EDSAC 2 assembler designed by D. J. Wheeler in the early nineteen-fifties. An elegant subroutine which allows the rules for formation of text items to be specified by table has been described by Cooper[14], and an expository treatment of this approach has been given by Day[15].

4.7 Symbol definition

Symbols can be defined either by appearing in the label field or by appearing on the left of a SET or EQU pseudo-operation. Symbols defined as labels are easiest to deal with. In the first pass they are merely entered in the symbol table with a value determined by the location counter, and type 'relative' (since the location counter is counting from zero at the beginning of the routine). The form of the symbol table entry is:

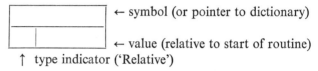

← symbol (or pointer to dictionary)

← value (relative to start of routine)

↑ type indicator ('Relative')

Note that if multiple location counters are used the 'value' field must also indicate to which location counter the address is relative. Symbols defined by an EQU operation initially have a table entry of the form:

left symbol	
	right symbol

↑ type = 'EQU'

This entry is further processed by a post-scan at the end of Pass 1, when the second part of the entry (symbol on right of EQU) is replaced by a pointer to the table entry for that symbol, so that all symbols defined as equivalent to each other are linked on a chain. (Note that the chain has to be constructed at the end of Pass 1, since the hash table might be expanded during the operation of Pass 1, invalidating any pointers to other entries.) If a symbol is defined by a SET operation, the expression on the right of the SET is evaluated to give the value and mode (relocatable or absolute). This evaluation process is basically identical with that used in Pass 2, which will be described later. However, in Pass 2 all symbol values are known; in evaluating in Pass 1 the expression must not contain any symbols that have not yet been defined.

The post-scan of the symbol table at the end of Pass 1 has already been mentioned. Besides setting up the equivalence chains, this serves the additional purpose of constructing the definition table.

Setting up the equivalence chains is more complicated than might appear at first sight. The symbol table is scanned, looking for entries with type EQU. When one is found, there are a number of possibilities to consider, depending on the nature (local or global) of the two symbols involved. These are as follows:

(i) The right-hand symbol does not have an entry in the symbol table. In this case the entry in the symbol table is deleted, and instead a loader directive is output, which will effect the equivalence at load time (see Chapter 5). Deleting the entry from the symbol table ensures that the symbol will be treated as external by Pass 2.

(ii) The right-hand symbol has an entry in the symbol table, and neither symbol appears in the definition table. This is the easy case; the chain is set up in the symbol table in a straightforward manner.

(iii) The right-hand symbol has an entry in the symbol table, and both symbols appear in the definition table. The chain is set up both in the symbol table and in the definition table.

(iv) The right-hand symbol appears in the symbol table and one of the symbols appears in the definition table. The other symbol is copied into the definition table, and the chain is set up in both tables as in the previous case.

4.8 The pseudo-operation table

This table is constructed on the same lines as the symbol table, except that the 'value' recorded in the table is the address of a subroutine to be entered to process the pseudo-operation in question.

4.9 Pass 1 flow chart

Fig. 4.1 shows the flow of control through Pass 1; with its annotations and the discussion given so far, it should be self-explanatory.

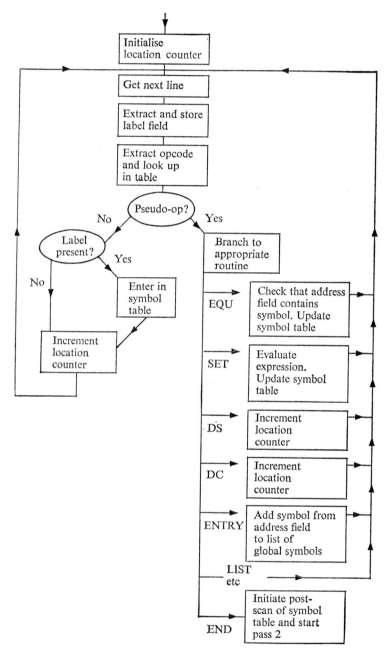

Fig. 4.1. Flow chart for Pass 1 of assembly

41

4.10　The second pass

Symbol Tables for Pass 2. Pass 2 has available to it two symbol tables. The first is the symbol table constructed in Pass 1. The second is an opcode/pseudo-op table in which each entry has the form:

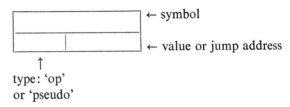

type: 'op'
or 'pseudo'

Whilst Pass 2 is operating it builds up the use table and the product use table for use during the link-editing and loading phase. The structure of these tables has already been described.

Strategy for Pass 2. The main function of Pass 2 is to produce a binary-symbolic version of the routine together with relocation information, and to build up the use table and product use table. To fix ideas, let us suppose for the moment that we are generating code for a 24-bit machine, and that the function occupies six bits. For each instruction, therefore, we produce five six-bit characters: one for the function, three for the addrees, and one to indicate whether relocation is required. (This is an output format conveniently suited, for example, to a magnetic tape system that writes six-bit characters.) For a data word we again produce five characters: four to represent the 24 bits of data, and one for special indications: this can indicate, for example, relocation relative to more than one base so that tables of literals, etc., can be built up.

In processing a line of code the label field is ignored, since it was completely processed in Pass 1. (It will, however, be listed at this stage.) The opcode is then read and the operation table consulted. If the symbol is a genuine opcode its six-bit translation is output (through some blocking routine that does not concern us here); if it is a pseudo-op control it is switched according to the table entry; and if the symbol is not in the table an error message is output on the listing. The address field is then evaluated to generate an 18-bit quantity and relocation marker.

4.11 Evaluation of addresses

The address field consists of an operand-operator string; the textual analysis routine described earlier checks the syntactic correctness. The expression has to be arranged into the form

$$R + A \pm S_1 \pm S_2 \pm \ldots + P_1 + P_2 + \ldots + P_n$$

where R is a relative symbol, A is an absolute expression, the S_i are external symbols, and the P_i are products each of which involves at least one external symbol. R and A are completely evaluated; the S_i will produce entries in the use table, and the P_i will produce entries in the product use table.

We have already observed that the operators and operands are produced by repeated calls of the text item routine. An operand may be a constant or a symbol. If it is a constant it can be immediately evaluated; if it is a symbol, the symbol table is consulted and this will give one of three outcomes:

    (i) Symbol is in table with absolute value.
    (ii) Symbol is in table with relative value.
    (iii) Symbol is not in table—i.e. it is an external symbol.

If products of symbols are not allowed, the processing is simple. Constants and absolute symbols are accumalated to form component A; a relative symbol (there can be at most one) becomes the component R, and each external symbol is entered in the use table. If desired the mode of the non-external part can easily be checked at the same time using the rules given earlier. When products are allowed the situation is more complicated: an algorithm that will achieve the separation of an address into external and non-external parts, evaluating the non-external part, determining its mode, and producing entries in the use table and product use table for the external part is given as an Appendix.

(Similar processing is required in Pass 1 to evaluate expressions occurring on the right-hand side of a SET pseudo-operation. However, in that context external symbols are not allowed, and all local symbols must be defined. The modifications needed to incorporate these restrictions should be obvious.)

43

4.12 Action on pseudo instructions

$$\left.\begin{array}{l} \text{EQU} \\ \text{SET} \\ \text{ENTRY} \end{array}\right\} \text{ignore line (dealt with completely in Pass 1)}$$

DS   increase location counter appropriately

DC   call subroutine to convert constants; increase location counter

LIST etc set switches to control listing

END   initiate tidying-up routine; output definition table, use table and product use table.

4.13 Refinements

The above description has dealt with the assembly of straight-forward items. We now outline the implementation of some more sophisticated user facilities, including those described in Chapter 2.

Changing Opcodes. It is often convenient for the programmer to be able to define his own opcodes, particularly if the computer has a rich instruction repertoire. This can be done by a pseudo-operation OPDEF; for example

LDA OPDEF LAC

would define LDA as an opcode with the same meaning as LAC. The implementation is trivial, involving a simple updating of the opcode table.

Multiple Location Counters. Implementation of these is straight-forward. When a relative address is produced the relocation informa-tion must specify the location counter in use at the time.

Symbol to Denote Current Location. If a symbol (e.g. asterisk) is used to denote the current location, the text item routine must recog-nise this as an operand, and the evaluation routine must be given the current value of the location counter as OP, with MS = 1 (i.e. relative symbol). Since the recognition is done as part of the 'get operand' sequence, a combination such as *** would be correctly interpreted as (current location)^2, and hence illegal.

4.14 Literals

A literal operand is recognised by characteristic warning symbol at the start of the address field. The first action of the assembler is to convert the operand to binary. A table is maintained containing all the literal operands that have occurred in the current routine: this table is searched and if a new literal is not found in the table it is added at the end. Thus duplication of constants in the table is avoided and a literal can be uniquely identified by its position in the table. This value is output as the address of the instruction, marked as relocatable with respect to the location counter assigned to literals. At the end of the routine the literal table is output along with the other symbol tables.

4.15 Complex instruction formats

We have considered only a simple two-field instruction. More complex instruction formats will commonly be encountered. To cater for these, the address field is generalised to allow the form:

expression,expression,expression, . . . , expression

where each expression is made up of symbols, constants and operators. The routine which processed addresses now becomes 'Read Expression', and evaluates an expression which is terminated by a comma or end-of-line. Some subfields, e.g. index register fields, may not sensibly have relative values, and some may not be allowed to include external symbols, so the 'read expression' routine must be provided with switches that can be set to indicate which sorts of symbol are acceptable. If external symbols are allowed in fields that do not extend to the rightmost end of the word, the use table must include the offset, so that the linkage editor can shift values appropriately before inserting them in instructions.

There are several cases to be distinguished:

(i) *Fixed instruction format and length.* This is the easiest case, and is typical of a word-oriented machine. The assembler includes

45

a table which gives the width and offset for each field. For example, on the Atlas computer, instructions have four fields, thus:

F	I_1	I_2	S
10	7	7	24

The generalised address field now consists of three subfields (F is the opcode), and the table is made up as follows:

Field	Width	Offset
I_1	7	31
I_2	7	24
S	24	0

In assembling this type of instruction, the read expression routine is entered a fixed number of times. After each entry the field table is consulted and the width is checked (or masked); the result is then shifted left by the amount of the offset and added into the part-assembled instruction. If undefined (external) symbols are allowed, the offset is copied from the field table into the use table.

(ii) *Variable instruction format, fixed instruction length.* In some word-oriented machines, the interpretation of the instruction as a number of fields depends on the opcode. For example, in the ICL 1900 series arithmetic instructions have the format

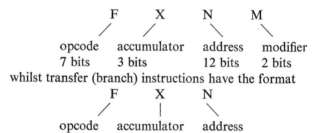

whilst transfer (branch) instructions have the format

F X N
opcode accumulator address
6 bits 3 bits 15 bits

To deal with this sort of structure, the opcode table must include an indicator specifying the appropriate instruction format; this can select an entry in a table that gives for each format the field widths and offsets.

(iii) *Variable instruction format, variable instruction length.* This is typical of byte-oriented machines, e.g. the IBM System 360.

There is no question of offset, since successive fields occupy successive bytes. The opcode table must still specify the format, but the information required is now the number of fields and their widths.

It can be seen that once the idea of a format table has been incorporated, it is easy to deal with diverse instruction formats. This is the germ of the idea of the *meta-assembler* that is described in more detail in Chapter 8.

4.16 Conditional assembly

The implementation of the simplest form of conditional assembly, the pseudo-operations IFF and IFT, is very straightforward. The values of the symbols (which must be defined) are obtained from the symbol table, the value of the relation is computed, and dependent on this the next line of code is or is not included. It is necessary to perform this operation in Pass 1 and Pass 2. If the assembler allows multiple location counters, it is possible to deal with an IFF or IFT in Pass 1 even when the symbols are as yet undefined. The technique is to start using a new location counter at the point where the pseudo-operation occurs; all subsequent relative address symbols will be relative to this counter. At the end of Pass 1, when by definition all local symbols will have been defined, the relation can be computed, and dependent on the outcome the auxiliary location counter can be set relative to the beginning of the routine, and all symbols dependent on it updated. In Pass 2 the symbol values will be known, and the decision whether or not to include the line can be taken immediately.

The implementation of AGO and AIF is not much more complicated. In both passes, AGO causes lines of code to be ignored until a line with the relevant sequence symbol in the label field is encountered. For AIF, the relation is computed, and if it is true, lines of code are omitted until the specified sequence symbol is found. As before, by use of an auxiliary location counter it is possible to deal with an AIF in Pass 1 involving undefined symbols.

This chapter has by no means exhausted the subject. Any particular assembler will include some facilities that have not been discussed here. However, the reader should by now be in a position where he can make a reasonable attempt at working out how any special facility would be implemented.

5 Loaders and linkage editors

A loader does what its name implies; it loads programs into the computer store. We can distinguish three types of loader: *binary loaders, relocating loaders,* and *linking loaders.* A binary loader loads a complete program in absolute binary from some external device. A relocating loader takes a program in relocatable binary

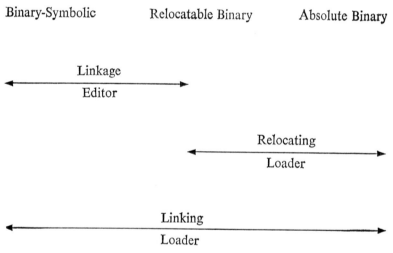

Binary-Symbolic   Relocatable Binary   Absolute Binary

Linkage
Editor

Relocating
Loader

Linking
Loader

Fig. 5.1. Components of a linkage and loading system

together with relocation information, and produces a program in core in absolute binary, having adjusted the relative addresses appropriately. A linking loader takes a number of routines in binary-symbolic form, and loads them into core as a single program, filling in cross references between routines and relocating as required. As already pointed out in Chapter 1, the filling-in of cross-references is logically distinct from relocation, and can be carried out independently by a linkage editor. In this case the output from the linkage editor is in a form suitable for loading by a relocating loader. The relationship between the various forms of loader is shown in Fig. 5.1.

5.1 Binary loaders

If a program is going to be used many times it is convenient to assemble it and then to output a binary dump or core-image on to some external medium, in order to save the time of assembly on future runs. Alternatively, a 'snapshot dump' of the core may be made after the program has been running for some time in order to provide a back-up point in case of later machine failure. In either case the binary loader is required in order to reinstate the core-image from the external medium. The loader is a trivial affair, such complication as there is arising from the need to check the accuracy of the information transferred to the store. This is usually achieved by dividing the binary into blocks, and applying a simple sum-check over each block. Commonly each block will be prefaced by the address at which it is to start. In this way it is possible to avoid loading large blocks of zeros representing empty store.

Many computers are provided with a bootstrap loader which can be brought into action by operating a switch on the control panel. This is usually a very simple binary loader capable of reading a fixed number of binary words into a fixed position in core. This is used to read in a more sophisticated loader.

5.2 Relocating loaders

The simplest relocating loader deals with the case of a single location counter. Relocation information may be distributed throughout the binary symbolic material, or may be collected at the end in the form of a map. In the first case the loader examines the flag associated with each incoming word to decide whether or not to add the relocation constant (i.e. the address of the start of the routine). When the routine is completed, the relocation constant is updated and the process continued with the next routine. If the relocation in-

49

formation is collected in a map, the loader first reads the routine and its map, thus:

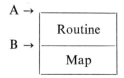

The map is then scanned and the specified words in the routine are relocated by having the address A added to them. Finally, the re-location constant is set to B, and the next routine and map are read into core, starting at B. (The routine will be preceded by a header which includes, inter alia, its length, thus allowing the point B to be determined.) A small complication may arise in the case of large programs from the need to find room in core both for the program being loaded and for the loader. One solution is to keep the loader in the space that will eventually be used for storage of data.

5.3 Common storage

So far we have assumed that the only external references in a routine are calls to other routines. Typically there will also be refer-ences to COMMON data areas. These can be dealt with by the use of a separate location counter (see below): alternatively, COMMON storage can be allocated backwards from the top of the store, thus:

Routine 1	Routine 2	→	←	Common Area

0   N

To facilitate this the assembler must include in the header of the compiled routine the names of the COMMON blocks used, and the loader builds up a storage allocation table giving the address of each COMMON block. It is necessary to adhere to the FORTRAN rule that named common blocks must be the same size in every routine that refers to them, and that blank COMMON, if used, must never exceed the size it had in the first routine loaded. Since all COMMON storage must be declared, the assembler can construct addresses relative to the start of the COMMON block, and the loader can relocate these accordingly.

5.4 Multiple location counters

These present no difficulty as far as relocation is concerned. Each binary word in the semi-compiled form is followed by a flag indicating which location counter the address is relevant to, and the appropriate relocation constant is added by the loader. The difficulty lies in initially setting the relocation constants. To illustrate the difficulty, consider the ICL 1900 system. Four different location counters are used, for lower data, program, upper data and literals The assembler records in the header of a routine the amount of store required relative to each location counter, but in order to set the relocation constants it is necessary to find the total size of each area by summing the requirements of each routine (including library routines). This means that loading becomes a two-pass operation.

5.5 Linkage editors and consolidators

We have seen that the use of multiple location counters forces a two-pass approach to loading. A common division of function is as follows:

> *First Pass*: Calculate total storage requirements for each area, incorporate library routines, and fill in external cross references, producing a complete program in relocatable binary on some external medium (usually disc).
> *Second Pass*: Load into core, relocating to produce absolute binary.

The first pass is commonly called *linkage editing* (IBM) or *consolidation* (ICL). Calculation of total storage requirements is a trivial operation: the main interest is in the cross-references between routines, that is, the use of external symbols.

51

5.6 Linkage editors

Each routine provides information about its use of global symbols in the Definition, Use and Product-Use tables described in Chapter 4. The linkage editor coordinates the cross-reference information in a *linkage symbol table* (LST for short), which includes details of all global symbols that have been defined or referred to in the program processed so far. The main section of the LST is organised as a hash table and each entry consists of two items, thus:

Name		
Tag	Mode	Value

'Name' is either the actual symbol, or a pointer to a dictionary entry (see Chapter 3). 'Tag' indicates whether or not the symbol is defined. If Tag = 0, the symbol is defined, 'value' is the value, and 'mode' records whether it is absolute or relocatable. If Tag = 1, the symbol has been referred to in advance of its definition, and 'value' is a pointer to the subsidiary part of the LST which records forward references. Since the number of references to any symbol is unpredictable, this part of the table is organised as a chained list. Each entry has the form:

Flag	Position	Pointer

'Position' is the position in the program where the reference occurred. 'Flag' is 0 or 1 according as the symbol value is to be added or subtracted, and the 'pointer' points to the next entry pertaining to this symbol, the end of the chain being marked in a characteristic manner, such as a negative pointer. Unused entries in the table are chained together in a free list in the usual way.

If equivalence operations are allowed, the LST also records these, A symbol defined by an EQU is given Tag = 2 in the LST, and 'value' points to the entry for the symbol on the right of the EQU. These entries must be dealt with specially if the hash table is expanded.

The LST is initially empty, and is updated as each routine is read. First, the definition table for the routine is merged into the

LST. For each entry in the definition table (referred to as DT henceforward) the procedure is:

(i) Find if symbol is in LST. If not copy definition into LST.
(ii) If symbol is in LST flagged 'undefined' copy value into LST, flag as defined, and fill in forward references, returning forward reference chain to the free space chain. In filling in forward references the mode of the symbol must be compared with the mode already recorded for the address, this latter being modified if necessary. Using A for absolute and R for relocatable, the rules for combining modes are:

$$A + A \to A \qquad A - A \to A$$
$$A + R \to R \qquad A - R \to FAULT$$
$$R + A \to R \qquad R - A \to R$$
$$R + R \to FAULT \qquad R - R \to A$$

(iii) Symbol in LST flagged 'defined'. A diagnostic message is output, and the definition is ignored.

When all the entries in the DT have been dealt with, the use table for the routine is merged into the LST. For each entry the procedure is:

(i) Find if symbol is in LST. If not, create a new entry, flagged undefined, and start a forward reference chain with the information from the use table.
(ii) Symbol in LST, flagged 'undefined'. The chain in the LST is extended by one item to accommodate the new forward reference.
(iii) Symbol in LST, flagged 'defined'. The value from the LST is incorporated in the program as specified by the use table. As before, the mode must be checked and adjusted if necessary.

When all entries from the use table have been processed, the next routine is read. (We are deferring temporarily discussion of the product use table.)

When all the routines have been processed, any outstanding forward references in the LST are either errors (probably due to misspelling of a symbol), or correspond to library routines. If there are

53

such forward references, the library is now scanned. If it consists of a series of routines in standard relocatable binary format, the loader as described will incorporate library routines that have been called and will fill in the address of the call instruction. Any forward references outstanding after the library has been scanned are definitely errors, and can be recorded in a suitable diagnostic. In the interests of efficiency, it is worthwhile counting the number of forward references before the scan of the library file is started, decrementing the count as forward references are dealt with, and terminating the scan if the count reaches zero.

Difficulties can arise if a library routine itself uses other library routines. If the library is searched in a linear scan, such dependent routines must come *after* the routine that calls them, otherwise they will never be incoporated. This may require that a particular routine occur in the library file in more than one place. If the library is held on disc, then the sensible thing to do is to keep a dictionary giving the location of all the library routines. The entries in the LST with outstanding forward references are then compared with the dictionary to see if they are library calls. This obviates a scan of the whole library looking for a routine that is in fact a misspelling, and also gets over the trouble with dependent subroutines. (Sensible, yes; but at least one well known system treats its disc as a tape and makes a serial scan of the library!)

5.7 Products of external symbols

Products of external symbols give rise to entries in the product use table, which have to be processed by the linkage editor. This processing can be quite complicated, but since products of external symbols are relatively rare, a crude technique will often suffice; such a technique is now described.

After the processing of the definition table and use table, the product use table (PUT) is scanned. For each symbol occurring, the LST is interrogated. If the symbol is not present in the LST, or if it is present but marked 'undefined', nothing is done at the moment. If the symbol is defined, however, then the PUT entry is amended; the reference to the symbol is deleted, and the absolute part is multiplied by the symbol value. (At this point the mode of the symbol should be checked, to avoid multiplying by a relocatable value.) When the entire PUT has been processed in this way it is scanned once again. Any entries which now consist only of an absolute part are dealt with immediately, by adding into the specified location, and the other entries are added to a *master products table* (MPT). When all the routines have been read, the MPT is processed in the same way as the PUT for each routine. At the end of this operation, there should be no entries left that are not just an absolute value; if there are, they indicate errors and a suitable diagnostic can be produced.

5.8 Directives

In the same way that a program includes pseudo-operations to control the operation of the assembler, the output from the assembler can include *directives* that control the action of the linkage editor. Such directives may also be inserted subsequent to assembly. Apart from the obvious directive to indicate the end of the whole program (which may also indicate the entry point to the program), directives are usually provided to manipulate and define symbols. Typical directives include:

DEFINE   to define new global symbols,
RENAME   to rename global symbols,
EQU   to establish equivalences between global symbols

5.9 Storage allocation

It is evident that the dimensions of COMMON arrays must be declared at compile-time. It is possible to design the system so that allocation of space to arrays is left until link-edit time. In the BAS loader[16], provision is made for *public arrays*, which can be accessed by more than one routine, to have dimensions assigned at load time. In the LST a new item is associated with each entry, called the *length*. A positive nonzero length indicates that the symbol names an array for which storage has been allocated; zero length indicates an array for which storage has not yet been allocated, and a negative length indicates that the symbol is the name of a routine or entry point.

Directives are provided to allow definition of symbols that give the length of an array; in general these will involve products, and so make use of the product use table.

5.10 Overlay programs

Overlaying is the name given to the technique whereby a program that is too large for the available core store is held on mass storage and divided into sections that are loaded in turn into the same area of store. Typically the routines of a program are grouped into a *permanent unit* and a number of *overlay units*. The available store is divided into a *permanent area* and one or more *overlay areas*. The permanent area holds the permanent unit, and at any one time, each overlay area holds one of a specified list of overlay units. (Thus two units allocated to the same area cannot be present in core simultaneously.) The permanent area will also hold the non-overlaid data areas thus providing a communication area for overlay units occupying different overlay areas.

Consolidation and loading of an overlay program goes in a number of stages. In the first stage each overlay unit is consolidated like a complete program. Its storage requirements are evaluated and cross-references filled in. The new feature is that calls to other routines have their address flagged as relative either to the start of their own overlay area (which is of course unknown at this time) or to the start of the permanent area.

The next stage is to determine the size of the overlay areas: the size of an area is evidently that of the largest unit that will occupy it. (If storage is allocated according to several location counters this maximising process is carried out for each class of storage.) Having determined the sizes of the overlay areas store can be allocated, and origins for each overlay area determined.

The final stage is one of loading. Each overlay unit is processed in turn, being relocated according to the origin previously computed, and the resulting absolute binary being written to mass storage. (Note that at this stage a unit need not be loaded into the store area it will actually be obeyed in.)

At the end of loading the permanent area is set up, and a table giving the mass storage address of each overlay unit, and its associated overlay area, is constructed. (The routines required to read and write overlay units will have been incorporated in the program by the usual library mechanism.)

5.11 Other facilities—the LSS loader

The loading and linking systems so far described cater for two sorts of symbol, those local to a routine and those global to the whole program. The LSS Loader[17] allows a more elaborate name structure, akin to the block structure of ALGOL. In the LSS system, routines can be associated into a named *group*. Within a group of

Main Group (Implicit)

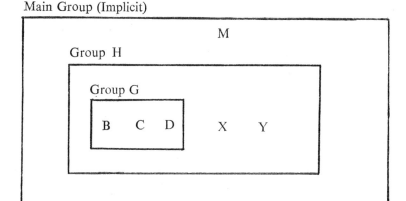

Fig. 5.2. Nested groups structure
(*M, B, C, D, X and Y represent routines*)

routines, a distinction is made between names local to one routine and those global over the group. Further, at the time that the group is defined, particular symbols can be specified to have a meaning outside the group. For example:

BLOCK GROUP A,B,C,U/V,W/Z

defines a group called BLOCK, and specifies that symbols A, B and C have the same meaning outside the group as inside, whilst symbols U and W have the meaning outside the group that is associated with symbols V and Z respectively inside the group. Further, groups can occur within other groups, thus providing a tree structure of names (cf. Fig. 5.2). Additional flexibility is provided by allowing explicit reference to symbols in other groups by a construction of the form BLOCK $ SYM, which stands for the symbol SYM in the group BLOCK if the reference appears immediately outside the group BLOCK. Fig. 6 shows a possible arrangement of groups, and Fig. 5.3

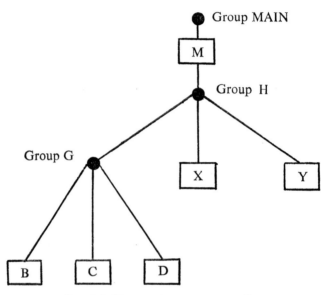

Fig. 5.3. Tree structure corresponding to nested groups of Fig. 5.2

shows the associated tree structure of names. In this tree, the terminal nodes represent routine names, and the other nodes are group names. In the main program. H$SYM stands for the symbol SYM in group H, whilst HGSYM indicates the symbol SYM in group G. It can be seen that the symbol name is preceded by group names which define a path through the tree; the construction ⟨group name⟩$ leads one level down. To allow completely general cross-referencing, $ on its own is used to indicate a reference one level up in the tree. Thus in routine B, the reference $$SYM would indicate symbol SYM in the main group. More elaborate constructions will define any path through the tree.*

The loader for such a system is substantially more complicated than the linkage editors so far described. The symbol table must contain all the tree structure; one consequence of this is that the loader becomes multipass, since it is necessary to make one pass to pick up all the group definitions, so as to set up the tree initially. The interested reader is referred to the paper already cited for full details of the implementation.

5.12 Load-time computation—the IAL loader

The straightforward linkage editor described earlier is an effective, but rather inflexible, instrument. The reader will already have noted the difficulties that arose in trying to cater for multiplication of external symbols. The IAL loader[18] operates on a rather different philosophy. It takes as its input a stream of binary words; some of these are treated as data to be placed in store, whilst others are treated as instructions, to be obeyed immediately. Such instructions may alter the contents of store, modifying information already read in, or may carry out calculations, or may set indicators which will affect the execution of later instructions. At any instant, the loader can be in one of two modes: *copy mode* or *instruction mode*. In copy mode, binary words are copied into store, whilst in instruction mode they are taken singly and interpreted as instructions for immediate execution. One instruction causes a switch into copy mode, either for a specified number of words, or until a recognisable *separator* is encountered.

A loader instruction consists of an operation and an operand, and is written on paper in the form F/N. There is a *loading pointer* S which points to the next register to be loaded; in copy mode S is incremented by 1 after each word has been copied into store. In addition there is a *base* B used for relocation. Simple relocating and loading is achieved with the following instructions:

* This tree structure of names, and the method of specifying paths through the tree, are very similar to a mechanism described by Mealy[11].

LR/0   load a record (i.e. up to the next separator) into consecutive storage registers starting at S; update S

LB/0   set B = S

ASB/m ⎱ add (subtract) value of B to (from) contents of
SSB/m ⎰ register B + m

Another group of instructions provide for the manipulation of symbols:

L/sym   set symbol = S

+P/sym   add value of symbol to register S − 1 (i.e. the register just loaded)

−P/sym   ditto, but subtract

+PR/sym ⎱ add value of symbol to register S − m
0/m ⎰

The usual facilities are provided for keeping track of forward references in these symbol manipulations.

A novel feature is the ability to perform elaborate computations at load time. This is achieved by using the store registers from S onwards as a stack, and providing an instruction FN/m which applies a function (identified by a code number m) to the two quantities in the topmost registers of the stack. Operations provided include all the arithmetic operations, logical operations, shifts and rotations, etc. It is thus possible to cope with addresses which include the full range of operations. All the assembler has to do is to convert the expression into reverse-Polish notation, which is the appropriate form for stack operation. In a similar way, elaborate calculations of symbol values can be performed.

The IAL loader includes many other interesting features; the reader is referred to the description already cited for further details.

5.13 Speeding up link-editing

A completely general linkage editor can be very slow in operation, and it is not uncommon to find a situation where more time is spent link-editing than is spent in compiling. Dramatic increases in speed can sometimes be achieved by tailoring the linkage editor to a particular class of job. As an example, we describe the FASTLINK system written by P. McManus of IBM for the System 360; this was written to link routines produced by a FORTRAN compiler, but the principle extends more generally. FASTLINK takes advantage of the fact that all FORTRAN programs make use of a particular group of library routines (input/output, standard functions, etc.). These are placed in the store in a fixed position, so that no library scan is needed to obtain them; moreover, any reference to them can be filled in immediately, thus reducing the number of forward references. The only situation that could cause trouble would be that in which the programmer wished to replace one of the standard functions by another of his own definition. If the programmer provides a routine called COS to replace the standard cosine function, with the system as described all calls to COS will be treated as calls to the standard routine in its fixed position, and the substitution will not take place. However, a simple device gets round this difficulty: if the programmer provides a routine with the same name as a standard routine, it is loaded as usual, and the entry point of the standard routine is overwritten by a jump to the programmer-defined routine. FASTLINK is very effective; in one installation it is reported[19] to have reduced link-editing time from a *minimum* of 25 seconds to a *maximum* of 5 seconds!

6 One-pass assemblers

Although the two-pass assembler is the most common form, one sometimes encounters assemblers that convert the source program in a single scan: these are called one-pass assemblers. The motivation for one-pass assembly can come from the two sources. If programs are typically small and frequently changed (as will occur for example in a University environment) there is an attraction in a fast load-and-go assembler that converts source material to absolute binary in a single pass. On the other hand, it may be desired to have independent compiling of routines on a small machine that does not have any backing store (mass storage). In this situation two-pass assembly requires that the source program be physically read twice over, and if the primary input device is slow (e.g. the paper tape reader on a Teletype) this is an intolerable burden (though at least one manufacturer imposes it, presumably in order to boost the sale of fast tape readers!).

One-pass assembly is practicable in the load-and-go situation because the whole of the binary program is present in core. This means that it is straightforward to back-track and fill in forward references as the relevant symbols are defined. This is exactly the same process as in the linkage editor; if a symbol has been referred to but not set, the symbol table entry points to the head of a chain of entries recording the occasions on which the symbol has been used.

If references to undefined symbols are allowed only when the symbol forms the entire address (i.e. if TRA END is valid, but TRA END + 1 is not valid if END is undefined), it is possible to use an elegant form of chaining devised by Wheeler[20]. Since the undefined symbol forms the whole address, until the symbol is defined the address part of the word can be used to hold the chain pointer. Thus the symbol table points to the most recent position that the symbol was used; this address part points to the preceding occurrence of the forward reference, and so on, the chain being terminated by placing some easily recognisable pattern in the address part of the last instruction.

An assembler of this kind will cope only with a straightforward source language and cannot, for example, deal with multiple location counters. The reason is that if you go from source to binary in one pass you cannot do any elaborate storage allocation on the way.

Typical of a one-pass assembler that produces binary-symbolic output is the PLAN assembler for the ICL 1900 series[21]. The PLAN source language requires that all data names be declared in advance, so that the forward reference problem arises only in connection with branch (control-transfer) instructions. (We only have to consider control transfers within a routine, since calls to other routines will be dealt with at link-edit time, as before, and can be left in symbolic form.) When a symbol is encountered in the address part of a branch instruction, the symbol table is examined. If it is a backward jump, the destination symbol will be in the table and the address can be filled in without further ado. If the symbol is not in the table (as will be the case for table the first forward jump to a particular label) it is entered in the symbol table with a value which consists of a marker to identify it and a unique serial number. An entry is also made in the *branch-ahead* table recording the position (relative address and location counter) of the branch instruction, and the serial number of the destination label (as recorded in the symbol table). If there are several forward jumps to the same point, on the second and subsequent occurrences the symbol will be found in the symbol table. Its special flag will indicate that is is a forward jump symbol, and the serial number will already be assigned, so that the entry in the branch ahead table can be made straightaway. Whenever a label is found the symbol table is consulted. If the symbol is present marked as a forward jump its true value is substituted, and loader directives are output that will cause the loader to backtrack and fill in the address at load-time. The relevant entries are then deleted from the branch-ahead table. Evidently, one-pass operation is achieved at the expense of postponing some of the work until load-time.

7 Macro assemblers

It often happens that a certain pattern of orders occurs in several places in a program, with only minor variations. This is particularly the case if there is a common operation that requires several machine orders for its execution, for example, the calling sequence for a call of another routine. Thus to call the routine SUB with parameters A and B it might be necessary to write:

```
LDX    4,*
TFR    SUB
NOP    A
NOP    B
```

Evidently, it would be convenient for the programmer to be able to write:

```
CALL   SUB,A,B
```

and have the calling sequence generated for him. The advantages of this approach are threefold. The programmer writes less, his program is more readable, and if at some future stage the calling sequence is changed, a change at one place in the program will ensure that all CALLs are changed without the need to alter each one individually.

A macro assembler allows the programmer to define *macro instructions* as sequences of ordinary instructions, and provides a means of inserting variable information in the generated sequences. Let us now describe a simple macro assembler; we will only be concerned with the new aspects, and it can be assumed that the assembler includes all the facilities that were previously described.

To define a macro instruction, the programmer writes the pseudo-operation **MACRO** in the operation field the macro name in the label field, and a list of *formal parameters* in the address field, for example:

```
CALL   MACRO  A,B,C
```

He follows this by a number of lines of code, the *macro body*, which may include instances of the formal parameters, and terminates the whole by the pseudo-operation MEND, thus:

```
CALL  MACRO  SUB,A,B
      LDX    4,*
      TFR    SUB
      NOP    A
      NOP    B
      MEND
```

Following this definition, he can use the macro in his program by writing its name in the operation field, and a list of *actual parameters* in the address field, for example;

```
CALL  BLOGGS, FO, FUM
```

When this *macro call* is encountered, the assembler substitutes the macro body, replacing the formal parameters by the corresponding actual parameters, so that if the call written above appeared, it would be replaced by:

```
LDX  4,*
TFR  BLOGGS
NOP  FO
NOP  FUM
```

The normal processes of assembly are then applied, as if the substituted material had actually been written in the program.

7.1 Implementation

7.1.1 Macro definition

Macro definitions are processed in pass 1. On encountering the pseudo-operation MACRO in pass 1 the assembler switches into *macro definition mode*, from which it will revert to normal mode on encountering MEND. When the assembler switches into macro definition mode it first creates a new entry in the *macro definition table*, and inserts the macro name in this entry; the formal parameters are recorded in an auxiliary list. Lines of code are then read and copied into the macro definition table, the only processing being to look for occurrences of the formal parameters, and to replace these by special identifiers of the form $@n$ (this standing for 'the nth parameter'). Thus the CALL macro defined above would appear in the table as follows:

```
name:  CALL
body:  LDX    4,*
       TFR    @1
       NOP    @2
       NOP    @3
```

7.1.2 Macro expansion

When a macro is used (or *called*) the assembler has to replace the call by the definition text, suitably modified by the insertion of actual parameters in place of formal parameters. This process of *macro-expansion* must take place in both pass 1 and pass 2, though in practice it is often convenient to avoid expansion in pass 2 by having pass 1 insert the expanded form in the output stream handed on to pass 2. Since macro-expansion involves scanning character strings there is usually a saving in time by only doing it once. (This method assumes that the assembler has access to a disc or magnetic tape to convey information between passes. If the source program is read from the external medium on each pass, as is the case on small machines, then expansion must necessarily be done twice.) Macro expansion in pass 1 is necessary in order to keep track of the location counter(s). It might seem that this could be avoided by storing the length of the macro in the definition table, but this would mean that nested macros were not possible, nor could we have labels in macros.

Let us assume that expansion takes place in pass 1 only. The assembly process is modified as follows. When the operation field is being processed, the symbol occurring therein is first sought in the macro definition table; if it does not occur there the pseudo-operation and opcode tables are examined as usual. (The sequence is important; doing things this way allows the programmer to replace basic machine operations by small groups of orders. For example, as a diagnostic aid it is possible to define all store orders as macros, which expand into groups of orders that check the address of the store order for validity.) If the symbol in the operation field appears in the macro definition table, the actual parameters are recorded in an auxiliary list, and the assembler switches into macro expansion mode. In this mode, the assembler is fed from the macro definition table instead of from the source program, and whenever the combination $@n$ is encountered, the appropriate actual parameter is inserted. At the end of the macro body, the assembler switches back to normal mode. Since macro definitions are completely processed in pass 1 they can be deleted from the source text handed on to pass 2.

Some assemblers have a number of macros built in; these are often called system macros. In order to allow the programmer the option of redefining these, the macro definition table must be examined by a linear scan starting with the most recent entry.

7.2 Nested macro calls

There is an obvious advantage to be gained from allowing the macro body to contain calls of other macros. Indeed, without this ability to nest macro calls, much of the usefulness of a macro assembler vanishes. The additional complication in the implementation is not very great. Instead of simply distinguishing between normal mode and macro expansion mode, it is necessary to define the state of the assembler by a *level number*. Level 0 corresponds to the previous normal mode, and the level is increased by 1 for each partially completed macro call. Thus when a macro name is recognised in the opcode field the action is as follows:

> If level $= 0$, set level $= 1$ and enter macro expansion mode as before.
> If level $\neq 0$, then:
> (i) Preserve the current set of actual parameters and the position reached in the current macro definition (i.e. the position in the macro definition table) on a stack.
> (ii) Increase level number by one.
> (iii) Copy the new actual parameters into the auxiliary list and start expansion of the new macro.

When the end of a macro definition is reached, if the level is 1 it is reset to zero and normal mode resumed. Otherwise, the level is decreased by one, the actual parameters for the previous macro call and the pointer are recovered from the stack, and expansion of the previous macro is resumed. (See Barron[22] for an account of stacks.) It should be noted that when macro calls are nested, actual parameters may be handed from the outer level to the inner. For example, suppose a macro is defined as follows:

```
LARGER   MACRO    A,B
         LAC A
         SUB B
         TFP * + 2            (transfer if positive)
         ZAC                  (zero accumulator)
         ADD B
         MEND
```

This macro selects the larger of its two arguments and leaves it in the accumulator. We can now define another macro, LARGEST, which will select the largest of three arguments, as follows:

```
LARGEST   MACRO    A,B,C
          LARGER   A,B
          SUB C
          TFP * + 2
          ZAC
          ADD C
          MEND
```

Now suppose we have in a program a call of LARGEST:

```
LARGEST   X,Y,Z
```

The expansion of LARGEST will start with actual parameters X, Y, and Z. LARGER will be recognised as a macro name, and the level will be increased by one, stacking the actual parameters of LARGEST The parameters of LARGER will appear in the definition of LARG-EST as @1 and @2, and in this particular context must be replaced by values from the stack, not from the auxiliary list. It should also be noted that this mechanism would work if a macro body included a call of itself; however this would only be of practical use if the macro body included some conditional assembly to terminate the recursion.

7.3 Further macro assembler facilities

Default Values. It is often useful to be able to specify a value that is to be taken if an actual parameter is omitted. One way of specifying this is as follows. Consider the definition:

```
EXAMPLE   MACRO   A,B = 5,C
          LAC A
          ADD B
          STO C
          MEND
```

Now consider the following calls:

EXAMPLE 1,2,3	EXAMPLE 1,,3	EXAMPLE 1,2
generates	*generates*	*generates*
LAC 1	LAC 1	an error message
ADD 2	ADD 5	
STO 3	STO 3	

Implementation of this facility merely requires a little extra information to be stored in the macro definition table.

Keywords. In the macro system just described parameters are identified by position in a list so that if a parameter is omitted two consecutive commas have to appear. A convenient facility for the user which permits parameters to appear in any order (or not at all), is obtained by making the items in the actual parameter list take the form:

formal name = actual value

For example for a call of the macro LARGEST defined above we could write:

```
     LARGEST   A = PIG,B = DOG,C = CAT
or   LARGEST   C = CAT,A = PIG,B = DOG
etc.
```

To implement this facility, it is necessary to retain the formal parameter names in the macro definition table (possibly with default values); when the macro is called these names are compared with the keywords in the actual parameter list in order to set up the table of actual parameters.

69

7.3.1 Labels in macros

Consider the following macro definition:

```
STORE   MACRO  A
        STO A
        TFP L          (transfer on plus)
        STZ A          (store zero)
L       NOP
        MEND
```

This contrived macro has the effect of a store order if the accumulator is positive, but stores zero in place of negative quantities. If this macro is called more than once there will be trouble, since the label L will be used more than once, leading to a multiple-definition error message. It is desirable that any labels appearing in a macro body should be systematically modified by the assembler to ensure that a unique label is generated at each call; this is readily done by maintaining a counter, N, which counts the number of macro calls, and appending the value of N to the labels in macro bodies. Thus, suppose a program contains two calls of the STORE macro, and these are the first two macro calls in the program, the generated code would include

```
        TFP    L0001
        STZ    ---
L0001   NOP
```

the first time, and

```
        TFP    L0002
        STZ    ---
L0002   NOP
```

the second time. A similar device can be employed to generate unique names for temporary storage registers.

7.3.2 Conditional assembly in macros

Conditional assembly features can be very valuable in a macro body, particularly if they allow testing of actual parameters. For example, suppose that it is required to define a macro MOVE, such that MOVE A,B transfers the contents of A to B; and suppose that we wish to be able to write AC (with the usual meaning) as an argument for the MOVE macro. The code we wish to generate is illustrated in the following examples:

```
MOVE X,Y      STO TEMP
              LAC X
              STO Y
              LAC TEMP

MOVE AC,Y     STO Y

MOVE X,AC     LAC X
```

This is achieved by the following definition:

```
MOVE    MACRO   A,B
        AIF     (A .NE. AC)  .SS1
        STO     B
        AGO     .SS2
.SS1    AIF     (B .NE. AC)  .SS3
        LAC     A
        AGO     .SS2
.SS3    STO     TEMP
        LAC     A
        STO     B
        LAC     TEMP
.SS2    MEND
```

(This definition could be simplified by introducing a new pseudo-operation MEXIT, which means 'end macro expansion as if the end of the definition had been reached'. This would replace AGO .SS2 in the example.) This facility is particularly useful when preparing programs for a compatible range of machines, since by changing one parameter quite different code can be generated to suit different configurations.

7.3.3 Concatenation

Arguments may not only be substituted in specified fields in the macro body, but may also be concatenated with character strings in the body. The period is used as a concatenation operator. Thus if the body includes the string HEAD.BASE, and HEAD is a formal parameter, the value of the formal parameter HEAD will be concatenated with the string 'BASE' when the macro is used. This makes it possible to use macros in which the arguments are inserted into complex expressions. For example,

```
SKIP   MACRO  N
       TFR        N. + * + 1
       MEND
```

The call SKIP 3 will be replaced by TFR 3 + * + 1, which is a relative jump which skips the next three instructions.

7.3.4 Variable number of arguments

Some macro assemblers provide a system variable whose value is the number of arguments in the particular call. Together with conditional assembly features this permits variable numbers of arguments to be dealt with. This facility usually appears in conjunction with a notation for referring to actual parameters by their numeric position in the argument list.

7.3.5 Global variables

Conditional assembly uses local variables within a macro body. Some assemblers provide global variables also. With these, it is possible to make the code generated for a particular call depend on what happened in some previous call. This makes it possible, for example to write a macro that will pick up an argument from a processor register if a flag is set, so that redundant STORE-LOAD combinations can be avoided.

7.3.6 Attributes

Attribute facilities provide a means of obtaining information about an actual parameter (e.g. it is a string, an integer, a floating-point number, etc) so that the code produced can be optimised.

The IBM OS/360 assembler has probably as wide a range of macro facilities as any modern assembler, and the reader is referred to the appropriate manual[23] for more details. For a good account of the ways in which macro facilities can be exploited, see Kent[24].

7.4 Macro assemblers and macro processors

Although the macro facilities are an integral part of a macro assembler, logically there is a clear distinction between the operation of macro expansion and the rest of assembly. This is apparent from the way in which the assembler operates when in macro expansion mode—the only essential difference between this and normal mode is the source of the code to be assembled. A macro processor permits the definition and expansion of macros as a purely textual operation, divorced from any particular assembler or compiler. Used as pre-pass to an existing assembler the macro processor is exceedingly powerful, since it allows individual fields in instructions to be generated by macro expansion. The interested reader is referred to the writings of Brown[25], Halpern[26] and Strachey[27] for further details.

8 Meta-assemblers

Assemblers for different machines have much in common. They organise symbol tables, evaluate expressions and generate binary words from a number of symbolic fields. The idea of a meta-assembler is to provide a system with these general capabilities, together with a means of describing (in machine-independent form) the assembly rules for a particular machine. The meta-assembler accepts this description and then functions apparently as a normal assembler. It evidently has much in common with a compiler-compiler[28]—indeed, it is not without significance that the originators of the Manchester Compiler-Compiler[29] entitled their first paper on the subject 'An Assembly Program for a Phrase Structure Language'.

The idea of a meta-assembler originated with Ferguson, who produced the only published paper on the subject[30]. The ideas described in the paper were utilised in the METASYMBOL assembler for the SDS 900 series, in the SLEUTH II and UTMOST assemblers for the UNIVAC 1107/8, and in the META system for the CDC 3300. This latter system is used for the illustrations in this chapter.

An important feature of these systems (which is usually glossed over in their descriptions) is that the syntax of the input to a meta-assembler is fixed. The meaning of the symbolic information can be defined by the user, but he cannot change the syntax. Thus although it is possible, using a meta-assembler, to write an assembler for most machines, it is not possible to mimic an existing assembler. (This is one of the many differences between a meta-assembler and a compiler-compiler.)

The essentially new features of a meta-assembler are:

and

    (i) the provision of compile-time procedures and functions

    (ii) a mechanism whereby the programmer can define the binary format to be generated for any instruction.

Superficially the input to META (we are now referring to the CDC implementation) looks like input to any assembler: each line has three fields—label, operation and operand.

The label is optional: if there is a symbol in this field it is assigned a value equal to the current location counter value. The operation may be the name of one of the built-in system operations (defined later); if it is not, it is assumed to be the name of a procedure, and this named procedure will be obeyed taking the operand field as an argument. (This is like a macro, but instead of textual substitution we obey a piece of program *written in assembly language*. This may itself contain calls to other procedures.)

The operand field contains an expression or group of expressions, made up of symbols and/or constants. These are evaluated by the META system in the same way that a normal assembler evaluates its address field. Unlike a normal assembler, the expressions may contain calls to user-defined functions.

A group of expressions separated by commas is called a *set*. META allows these to be nested in the operand field.

8.1 Symbol definition

A symbol acquires a value implicitly by appearing in a label field. Symbols can be set explicitly by directives thus

Symbol **NSET** set of expressions
Symbol **EQU** expression
Symbol **RDEF** expression

Symbols defined by EQU cannot be changed: symbols defined by RDEF can be changed. RDEF can also be used to redefine an element of a set, for example

E   NSET 3,5
.
.
.
E[2] RDEF 6

8.2 Control of binary output

The operation UNIT defines the vital statistics of the object machine. Thus

UNIT *b,w*

specifies that the byte size is *b* bits, and the word contains *w* bytes.

The basic operations for output of binary material are GEN and GENB.

GEN set

outputs the values of the expressions in the set as successive words, whilst GENB outputs the values in consecutive bytes. Thus

GENB 5, 7, 34, 10

would output 4 bytes. If the byte size were 6 bits the octal output would be 05074212.

A multiple field output can be defined by a FORM operation. For example, suppose we have a 24-bit machine with the following instruction format:

Opcode   6 bits
Index   3 bits
Address   15 bits

Then

INSTR   FORM 6,3,15

defines a template called INSTR which can subsequently appear as an operation: it will expect an operand which is a set of 3 elements. Thus

INSTR   LDA, 7, ALPHA + 1

will output a 24-bit word made up by evaluating the three set elements, truncating, shifting and assembling according to the template. Note that this allows us to write an expression as the operation code of an instruction (!)

8.3 Control facilities

META includes facilities for conditional and repetitive assembly: these do not differ in substance from the facilities already described in other assembly systems.

8.4 Procedures and functions

We have seen above that we can define a FORM corresponding to an instruction, and use this to generate instruction words. Obviously the programmer will not wish to write all his instructions in this form, so another mechanism, the *procedure*, is introduced. A procedure is a piece of assembly language like a subroutine, except that it is obeyed at compile time when its name appears in an operation field. A procedure may be quite complicated (a user-defined pseudo-operation) or it may consist only of a call for a FORM. For example we might write

```
        PROC   P
LDA     NAME
        INSTR  O'10', P[1], P[2]
        ENDS
```

(ENDS marks the end of a procedure definition)

This syntactically revolting bit of code defines a procedure called LDA: the P after PROC is the formal parameter which identifies the arguments that will follow the name when the procedure is called. The body of the procedure is a call on the previously defined FORM called INSTR: we have assumed the octal code for LDA is 10. Having made this procedure definition the programmer could use expressions like

LDA   7,   ALPHA + 1

which look very like normal assembler input. It would be tedious and uneconomical to define separate procedures for each machine operation: fortunately the system allows multiple entries to procedures. Thus suppose we have the following opcodes:

```
LDA   10
ADD   11
SUB   12
MPY   13
etc.
```

a suitable procedure definition would be as follows

```
OPC   PROC   P
LDA   NAME   O'10'
ADD   NAME   O'11'
SUB   NAME   O'12'
MPY   NAME   O'13'
      ---
      ---
      INSTR  OPC[1], P[1], P[2]
      ENDS
```

The multiple names are given on successive NAME lines, with octal equivalents. The set on the name line is assigned on entry to the symbol given in the label field of the PROC line (it would be difficult to produce a more confusing convention) thus if the assembler encounters MPY as an operation it will enter this procedure as if the line

```
OPC   RDEF   O'13'
```

appeared at its head.

Function definitions are similar to procedure definitions: they are introduced by the word FUNC, and the ENDS line must contain an expression in its operand field which is the value returned by the function. Functions are expected not to have side-effects, i.e. they do not generate code. As an example of their use, the following function has a value which is the next multiple of 128 above its argument.

```
        FUNC   P
NM128   NAME
V       RDEF   (P[1] + 127) ** O'77777600'
        ENDS   V
```

(** is the logical 'AND' operator: O introduces an octal constant). As an example of the use of this function, in a paged machine we might wish at some point to ensure that the location counter is advanced to a multiple of 128: this is done by

ORG   NM128[$]

ORG is a built-in operation to set the location counter. $ stands for the current value of the location counter.

8.5 Other facilities

Assistance in constructing an assembler is provided by the attribute functions, which allow the user to find out

 – if an expression is relocatable or absolute
 – the type of an object (e.g. integer, string, address, etc.)
 – the number of elements in a set
 – the number of bytes needed to contain the value of an expression

Another useful facility is the built-in function SYM, which causes the value of its argument to be used as a symbol. This makes it possible to construct an assembler in which the symbols do not follow the rules of META.

For example,

AB$2   RDEF   5

would be illegal, because AB$2 is not a valid META symbol, but

SYM('AB$2')   RDEF   5

would be acceptable.

Given a meta-assembler, writing an assembler for a new machine is merely a matter of writing procedures to correspond to the desired instruction and data formats. Since most computers have fairly limited number of different formats, this is a relatively rapid process. In view of this it is surprising that the technique has not been more widely adopted. Probably the main reason is the scarcity of published material on the technique, and the fact that what has appeared is not particularly explicit. Meta-assemblers introduce some useful ideas that may well find their way into ordinary assemblers. The most important are the provision of assembly-time procedures and functions, and the use of nested sets to specify operands.

9 Algol-like assemblers

At this point we should perhaps ask the question 'why are assemblers still used?' High level languages are adequate for many problems, but one needs to resort to assembly language if it is desired to have a close control over store allocation and to have direct control over the machine's internal registers. Thus assembly language finds its main use in the writing of operating systems and similar system software. In order to have direct control at the internal register level an assembly language program is necessarily written at a fine level of detail, with each instruction representing a single primitive operation. An unfortunate effect of working at this level of detail is that programs are rarely perspicuous: it is impossible to write an assembly language program that displays clearly the structure of the underlying algorithm.

Recently there has been a development in the direction of 'high-level' or 'Algol-like' assembly languages which attempt to combine fine control over machine registers and store with a structure that reflects the overall structure of the program, for example repetition loops, conditional statements, functions and procedures, etc. The facilities provided in such a language must correspond fairly closely to the actual hardware: for example, we cannot include anything that depends on dynamic storage allocation if the underlying hardware does not provide such facilities. (Put another way, the compiler for an Algol-like assembly language cannot assume the existence of a 'run-time system'. Every source statement except a procedure call must compile into open code.) The precise facilities provided in a system will depend on the particular machine. Typically they will include the following.

(i) Symbolic names (identifiers) with associated types. The types will correspond to the storage units manipulated by the machine instructions, for example on the IBM System

360 they would include *byte, short integer, integer, real* and *long real.*

(ii) Reserved identifiers for machine registers. A synonym facility may also be provided to associate other names with registers.

(iii) Block structure, giving scopes to identifiers.

(iv) Conditional and compound statements.

(v) One-dimensional arrays (but not multi-dimensional arrays —these cannot be accessed by simple indexing on most machines).

(vi) Procedures and functions. (Usually only one parameter will be possible, and the calling mechanism will be the FORTRAN call-by-address. This corresponds to passing the parameter as an address in an accumulator or general-purpose register.)

(vii) Simple expressions (but nothing involving temporary storage—all operators are of equal precedence and evaluation is by a simple left-to-right scan).

(viii) Provision for including basic assembly language (e.g. for input output operations).

The first high-level assembler was the PL 360 system described by Wirth in a classic paper[31]. As its name implies it is designed for the IBM System 360 machines. An Algol-like assembler for a small machine has been developed at the National Physical Laboratory: it is described by Wichman[32, 33]. Called PL516 it is designed for the Honeywell DDP516.

The flavour of an Algol-like assembly language can be obtained from Fig. 9.1, which shows a PL516 procedure to convert an integer from binary to decimal. Line numbers have been added to facilitate commentary.

Line 1: @. PROCEDURE indicates that this is an *accumulator procedure.* When it is called its argument will be in the accumulator, that is it will appear as a function in some other PL516 statement

Lines 2–4 are fairly straightforward. '255 is an octal constant, being the ASCII code for minus sign. The array dimension is negative because the hardware provision for loop control counts towards zero from a negative initial value

```
 1.    @ .PROCEDURE CONVERT;
 2.      .INTEGER N, T, COUNT;
 3.      .CONSTANT MINUSCHAR = '255;
 4.      .ARRAY POWERS[-5] ( 10 000, 1 000, 100, 10, 1 );
 5.      .BEGIN
 6.      .IF @ .LZ .THEN
 7.        .BEGIN
 8.        N = .NEG @;
 9.        DEC[-6] = MINUSCHAR
10.        .END
11.      .ELSE
12.        .BEGIN
13.        N = @;
14.        DEC[-6] = SPACE
15.        .END
16.      .FOR # = -5 .DO
17.      .BEGIN
18.      T  = .POWERS[#];
19.      COUNT = .Z;
20.      .WHILE N .GE T .DO
21.        .BEGIN.
22.        T = T + POWERS[#];
23.        %IRS,COUNT
24.        .END;
25.      DEC[#] = COUNT + ZEROSYMBOL;
26.      N = N - T + POWERS[#]
27.      .END;
28.      .END;  & CONVERT
```

Fig. 9.1. Example of a PL.516 procedure. (Reproduced from "PL516, an Algol-like Assembly Language for the DDP516" by B. A. Wickmann [National Physical Laboratory C.C.U. Report 9, April 1970])

Lines 6–16: IF @.LZ means 'if accumulator less than zero'. .NEG is a unary operator which negates its argument, and DEC is a global array.

Line 16: # is an anonymous counting variable. 15 is the initia value of the count (see above)

Line 19: .Z stands for zero

Line 23: % introduces a basic assembler instruction. IRS adds 1 to store, skipping the next instruction if the result is zero. Since COUNT started at zero the skip will never take place. This is a piece of low cunning that has no place in a high-level assembler.

Line 25: This constructs the appropriate ASCII code for the decimal character whose value is COUNT.

High level assemblers are presently in their infancy. The gradual introduction of such systems foreshadows the end of assembly language programming as we have known it in the past. Few will mourn its passing.

Appendix

Evaluation of address field

The following algorithm evaluates an address field, separating absolute, relative and external parts, and computing the mode of the non-external part. Relevant tables are updated as the evaluation proceeds.

The address is assumed to include symbols, constants and the operators +, − and * only. It is converted in a single scan which at each stage includes an operand and the two operators on either side of it.

We use ⊢ and ⊣ to mark the beginning and end of an expression respectively. The variables involved are as follows:

VAL   accumulates the value of the nonexternal part

MODE   records the mode of the nonexternal part (0 = absolute, 1 = relative, anything else = malformed)

PR   is a flag that records whether a product is being recorded in the product use table (1 = yes, 0 = no)

TEMP   is used for temporary storage

OP
MS   these are set for each operand according to the table below
ES

	OP	MS	ES
constant	value	0	0
local symbol, absolute value	value	0	0
local symbol, relative value	value	1	0
external symbol	0	0	1

The process is initialised by setting VAL, MODE, PR and TEMP to zero. At each step the operand is evaluated, setting OP, MS and ES according to the table, and then action is taken according to the operators on either side. The action for the four essentially different contexts that occur is now given. Two commonly used procedures are first defined:

Check Relative Symbol:	*if MS* = 1, *mark expression as mal-formed and exit.*
Advance:	*if right operator is* ⊣, *exit, otherwise move scan to right to centre on next operand.*

(1) ⊦, ±
  ±, ±
  ±, ⊣

if *ES* = 1 **then** *enter symbol in use table and Advance* **else** *VAL*: = *VAL* ± *OP*; *MODE*: = *MODE* ± *MS*; *Advance*.
(*Choose* + *if left operator is* + *or* ⊦, *and* − *if left operator is* −.)

(2) ⊦, *
  +, *
  −, *

if *ES* = 1 **then** *start entry in PUT with absolute part* = ±1; *PR*: = 1; *enter symbol in PUT*; *Advance* **else** *Check Relative Symbol*; *TEMP*: = ± *OP*; *Advance*.
(*Choose* + *if left operator is* ⊦ *or* +, *and* − *if left operator is* −.)

(3) *, *

if *ES* = 1 ∧ *PR* = 1 **then** *enter symbol in PUT*; *Advance* **else if** *ES* = 1 ∧ *PR* = 0 **then** *start entry in PUT with absolute part* = *TEMP*; *PR*: = 1; *TEMP*: = 0; *Enter symbol in PUT*; *Advance* **else if** *ES* = 0 ∧ *PR* = 1 **then** *Check Relative Symbol; multiply absolute part of PUT entry by OP*; *Advance* **else** *Check Relative Symbol*; *TEMP*: = *TEMP**OP; *Advance*.

(4) *, ±
  *, ⊣

if *ES* = 1 ∧ *PR* = 1 **then** *enter symbol in PUT*; *Advance* **else if** *ES* = 1 ∧ *PR* = 0 **then** *PR*: = 1; *start entry in PUT with absolute part* = *TEMP*; *enter symbol in PUT*; *TEMP*: = 0; *Advance* **else if** *ES* = 0 ∧ *PR* = 1 **then** *Check Relative Symbol; multiply absolute part of PUT entry by OP*; *Advance* **else** *Check Relative Symbol*; *VAL*: = *VAL* + *TEMP* * *OP*; *TEMP*: = 0; *Advance*.

Bibliography

1 — 'IBM System/360 Operating System Assembly Language'. Form C28-6514-5. IBM (United Kingdom) Ltd.
2 — 'PDP7 Symbolic Assembler Manual'. Digital Equipment Corporation.
3 — 'Atlas 1 Programming Manual'. International Computers Ltd.
4 Morris, R. 'Scatter Storage Techniques'. *Commun. Assoc. Comput. Mach.,* Vol. 11, p. 38, 1968.
5 Braden, H. V. and Wulf, W. A. 'Implementation of a BASIC System in a Multiprogramming Environment'. *Commun. Assoc. Comput. Mach.,* Vol. 11, p. 688, 1968.
6 Day, A. C. 'Full table quadratic searching for scatter storage'. *Commun. Assoc. Comput. Mach.,* Vol. 13, p. 481, 1970.
7 Peterson, W. W. 'Addressing for Random Access Storage'. *IBM J. Res. Dev.,* Vol. 1, p. 130, 1957.
8 Schay, G. and Spruth, W. G. 'Analysis of a File Addressing Method'. *Commun. Assoc. Comput. Mach.,* Vol. 5, p. 459, 1962.
9 Hopgood, F. R. A. 'A Solution to the Table Overflow Problem for Hash Tables'. *Computer Bull.,* Vol. 11, p. 297, 1968.
10 Hext, J. B. 'Programming Languages and Compiling Techniques'. Ph.D. Thesis, Cambridge, 1956.
11 Mealy, G. H. 'A Generalised Assembly System'. RAND Corporation Report, reprinted in 'Programming Languages and Systems', edited by S. Rosen. McGraw Hill, New York, 1967.
12 Backus, J. W. *et al.* 'The FORTRAN Automatic Coding System'. *Proc. Western Joint Comput. Conf.,* Vol. 11, p. 188, 1957.
13 — Any one of the many introductions to FORTRAN currently available.
14 Cooper, B. E. 'Basic Subroutine for the Input of Numbers, Words and Special Characters'. *Computer J.,* Vol. 11, p. 157, 1968.
15 Day, A. C. 'The Use of Symbol State Tables'. *Computer J.,* Vol. 13 p. 332, 1970.
16 Curtis, A. R. and Pyle, I. C. 'A Proposed Target Language for Compilers on Atlas'. *Computer J.,* Vol. 5, p. 100, 1962.
17 McCarthy, J., Corbato, F. C. and Daggett, M. M. 'The Linking Segment Subprogram Language and Linking Loader'. *Commun. Assoc. Comput. Mach.,* Vol. 6, p. 391, 1963.

[18] Richards, M. and Whitby-Strevens, C. 'IAL Reference Manual., University Mathematical Laboratory, Cambridge, 1967.

[19] Samet, P. A. 'Software Requirements of Universities'. *Computer J.,* Vol. 11, p. 236, 1968.

[20] Wilkes, M. V., Wheeler, D. J. and Gill, S. 'Programs for an Electronic Digital Computer'. (2nd Edition.) Addison-Wesley, New York, 1957.

[21] — 'PLAN Reference Manual'. International Computers Ltd.

[22] Barron, D. W. 'Recursive Techniques in Programming'. Macdonald and Co., London, 1968.

[23] — IBM System/360 Operating System Assembler Language. Form C28–6514, IBM (United Kingdom) Ltd.

[24] Kent, W. Assembler Language Macro Programming *Computing Surveys,* Vol. 1, p. 183, 1969.

[25] Brown, P. 'The ML/I Macro Processor'. *Commun. Assoc. Comput. Mach.,* Vol. 10, p. 618, 1967.

[26] Halpern, M. 'XPOP: A Meta-Language without Meta-Physics'. *Proc. Fall Joint Comput. Conf.,* Vol. 26, p. 57, 1964.

[27] Strachey, C. 'A General Purpose Macro Generator'. *Computer J.,* Vol. 8, p. 225, 1965.

[28] Feldman, J. and Gries, D. 'Translator Writing Systems'. *Commun. Assoc. Comput. Mach.,* Vol. 11, p. 77, 1968.

[29] Brooker, R. A. and Morris, D. 'An Assembly Program for a Phrase-Structure Language'. *Computer J.,* Vol. 3, p. 168, 1960.

[30] Ferguson, D. E. 'The Evolution of the Meta-Assembly Program'. *Commun. Assoc. Comput. Mach.,* Vol. 9, p. 190, 1966.

[31] Wirth, N. 'PL 360, A Programming Language for the 360 Computers', *J. Assoc. Comput. Mach.* Vol. 15, p. 37, 1968.

[32] Wichmann, B. A., 'PL516, An Algol-like Assembly Language for the DDP 516' C.C.U. Report 9, National Physical Laboratory, 1970.

[33] Bell, D. A. and Wichmann, B. A., 'An Algol-like Assembly Language for a Small Computer', *Software Practice and Experience* Vol. 1, p. 61, 1971.

Index

Names of computers and languages are in capitals.